Only Believe!

By Jamie Dershem

WESTBOW®
PRESS
A DIVISION OF THOMAS NELSON
& ZONDERVAN

"By permission. From Merriam-Webster's Collegiate® Dictionary, 11th Edition ©2014 by Merriam-Webster, Inc. (www.Merriam-Webster.com)."
All Scripture is taken from the *King James Version* except where noted.
The NIV Textbook Bible, The Zondervan Corporation © 1984
Scripture quotations, footnotes, etc. marked NKJV are taken from the *Spirit-Filled Life Bible New King James Version* © 1991 by Thomas Nelson, Inc. Used by permission.
Scripture taken from *THE AMPLIFIED BIBLE*, Old Testament copyright © 1965, 1987 by the Zondervan Corporation; The Amplified New Testament copyright © 1958, 1987 by the Lockman Foundation. Used by permission. These will be marked AB.
The Message Remix (or MSG): The Bible in Contemporary Language, © 2003 by Eugene H Peterson

* * *

Please note that all words referring to deity, Heaven, the Word—Jesus, Grace and the Believer will be capitalized in *Only Believe!*, in honor and respect of Who He is—Holy; and the way we receive Him through Grace to become a Christian Believer in God's kingdom. I believe Heaven is a real place like Kalamazoo or California and should be capitalized, as they are, unless the verse does not capitalize it. Jesus said in John 6:38, "I came down from heaven . . ." Also note, that any reference to satan will not be capitalized, because he is a liar and deceiver, and does not deserve any respect.
"Dis-ease" is not a typographical error, but explains any *uncomfortable condition* in the body or life. It is a curse!

WestBow Press books may be ordered through booksellers or by contacting:

WestBow Press
A Division of Thomas Nelson & Zondervan
1663 Liberty Drive
Bloomington, IN 47403
www.westbowpress.com
1 (866) 928-1240

Because of the dynamic nature of the Internet, any web addresses or links contained in this book may have changed since publication and may no longer be valid. The views expressed in this work are solely those of the author and do not necessarily reflect the views of the publisher, and the publisher hereby disclaims any responsibility for them.

Any people depicted in stock imagery provided by Thinkstock are models, and such images are being used for illustrative purposes only.
Certain stock imagery © Thinkstock.

ISBN: 978-1-4908-5346-8 (sc)
ISBN: 978-1-4908-5347-5 (hc)
ISBN: 978-1-4908-5345-1 (e)
Library of Congress Control Number: 2014917418

Printed in the United States of America.
WestBow Press rev. date: 11/13/2014

Contents

I devote my first book to my closest Friend,
truest Guide and most precious Companion—the Holy Spirit.
Without His constant encouragement and help,
Only Believe could not have been written.

Only Believe was inspired by His love,
so that you could have a new powerful, healthy life.
Our greatest desire is that all that read *Only Believe*
will be able to handle life's daily challenges,
with the tools that God has made available in His Word,
to give you a confidence that
nothing is impossible with God
when you *Only Believe!*

This is the first day of the rest of your life!

I call heaven and earth to record this day against you,
that I have set before you life and death, blessing and cursing:
therefore choose life, that both thou and thy seed may live:
—Deuteronomy 30:19

How to use Only Believe!:

Read *Only Believe!* **out loud**, because "faith comes by hearing and hearing by the Word of God" (Rom. 10:17).

Receive the Word, because it is "life to those who find it and health to all their flesh" (Prov. 4:22 NKJV).

Apply it to your life. "Blessed (happy and to be envied) rather are those who hear the Word of God and obey and practice it!" (Luke 11:28 AB)

Meditate on each chapter until you can *stand* on that truth, and can say "I've got it!" Learn it so well that you can teach it.

As you find suggested faith confessions, mark them with a tab or write them down, and then **print them out to confess every day** until they are manifested. If you don't, the enemy will rob you of them, because satan comes immediately to take what was sown in your heart. (Mark 4:15)

Expect to be blessed as you read and **believe**, because I have prayed for all those that would read *Only Believe!*

Mark your calendar to read it again in six months.

Finally, by the extent and seriousness of your applying what you read, you will receive!

Only Believe!

Introduction

[Recommendation: Read this book out loud to yourself.]

Luke begins his Gospel with this statement:

> Forasmuch as many have taken in hand to set forth in order a declaration of those things which are most surely believed among us, even as they delivered them unto us, which from the beginning were eyewitnesses, and ministers of the word; it seemed good to me also, having had perfect understanding of all things from the very first, to write unto thee in order, most excellent Theophilus, that thou mightiest know the certainty of those things, wherein thou has been instructed.
>
> —Luke 1:1–4

I too have read many Christian books based on the Bible, testimonies of healings and miracles, besides what God has done for me, that I would like to share with you.

Another reason I began writing *Only Believe!* was for all those people that didn't believe when I prayed for them, even when the Holy Spirit gave evidence that He was present. Many years ago the Lord told me that "When I lay hands on the sick, they shall recover." I praise God that He has kept His word to me about this. Because I always use the Word when I pray and walk in faith (that both the enemy and the Lord has heard me), I'm always disappointed that the person didn't believe and receive their miracle. So I hope this book gets into the hands of those that doubted.

> These things we write to you that your joy may be full.
> —1 John 1:4 NKJV

The Bible says in Proverbs 4:7, "Wisdom is the principal thing; therefore get wisdom: and with all thy getting get understanding." And 3 John 2: "Beloved, I wish above all things that thou mayest prosper and be in health, just as your soul prospereth." So I'd like to show you the Scriptures which I have learned over the years, that have helped me, *and* that I continue to stand on. Regarding "stand" I mean confess regularly, at any time of the day, whether I am praying, praising, driving, cleaning the house—you get the idea.

Proverbs 4:20–22: "My son, attend to my words; incline thine ear unto my sayings. Let them not depart from thine eyes; keep them in the midst of thine heart. For they are life unto those that find them, and health to all their flesh." This book is for all those who need healing somewhere in their bodies, besides *how to use the Word for the rest of your life*. Notice this verse says "My son", so it is speaking to men, who should be the spiritual heads of the household. Most of the Bible is about men, leaders, kings, judges, disciples, and servants of the Lord, besides Jesus.

The Holy Spirit keeps prompting me to spend more time studying the Word on *healing* to receive the healing I need, so that is why I'm writing this book. "Then said Jesus to those Jews which believed on Him, If ye continue in my word, then are ye My disciples indeed; and ye shall know the truth, and the truth shall make you free . . . If the Son therefore shall make you free, ye shall be free[1] indeed" (John 8:31, 32, 36). Free of every symptom, pain or curse you had before you started reading this book.

One author shared that when he spent a week (1–8 hrs a day) preparing to teach a healing seminar, his symptoms disappeared. That's what I've shared with many people that need healing or a miracle: Give yourself a *healing seminar*, by spending extra time studying the Word on healing, health, and related topics, which you'll find in *Only Believe!* So I took this good advice, and began writing out Scriptures I knew, and kept adding others as I found them, or as the Holy Spirit led me, which was continually.

Only Believe! is written for all those that want to be healed and healthier, not for theologians. Many Scriptures given reveal *what is pertinent to receiving healing, protection* or *instruction*, and not the whole verse, which you can look up.

> For My thoughts are not your thoughts,
> neither are your ways My ways, saith the Lord.
> For as the heavens are higher than the earth,
> so are My ways higher than your ways,
> and My thoughts than your thoughts.
> —Isaiah 55:8, 9

Hosea 4:6: "My people are destroyed for lack of knowledge". . . God is omniscient—all knowing, which is one

---

[1] *Free*: Romans 8:2 NKJV, Strong's #1659: To liberate, acquit, set free, deliver. In the NT the word is used exclusively for Jesus' setting believers at liberty from the dominion of sin.

of the gifts of the Spirit: the word of knowledge. So to have more knowledge, we need to spend more time with the Lord and in the Word—one in the same.

Proverbs 10:21: "Fools die for lack of wisdom." The "word of wisdom" is another gift of the Spirit, which comes from God as He wills. James 1:5–8: "If any of you lack wisdom, let him ask of God, that giveth to all men liberally and upbraideth not; and it shall be given to him. But let him ask in faith, with nothing wavering. For he that wavereth is like a wave of the sea driven with the wind and tossed. For let not that man think that he shall receive any thing of the Lord. A double minded man is unstable in all his ways." So let's take care of this *lack* and *doub*t right now, and make you firm in your *belief* that *you* are healed through Jesus stripes, because nothing is impossible with God! (Luke 1:37)

> It is the Spirit who gives life . . . The
> words that I speak to you,
> they are spirit, and they are life.
> —John 6:63 NKJV

In the *DIY* series *Yard Crashers* on *Dish TV*, the landscape contractor finds someone who needs a new front or back yard landscape job free. He follows them to their house, looks over the situation, and asks them what they would like to see in that location. He makes some suggestions and tells them to get some helpers to be there the next day. Then he shows up bright and early the next morning with a plan, skilled help and supplies. Next, they "crash and trash" the owners yard, so they can begin the better plan for a beautiful yard, patio, etc.

What I want you to see is that you need to get rid of those old mind-sets, that have prevented you from going for the big plan God has for your life. As Jeremiah 29:11 NKJV says, "For I know the thoughts that I think toward you, says the Lord, thoughts of peace and not of evil, to give you a future and a hope." You see God can see all that is going on in your life and He knows how to get you from where you are (the weeds, the junk, the unfinished stuff and the poor choices you've made) to that beautiful, fulfilling life of health and wellbeing; where you can be blessed and be a blessing to others.

> For whatsoever things were written aforetime
> were written for our learning,
> that we through patience and comfort of
> the scriptures might have hope.
> —Romans 15:4

So if you want this book to really accomplish something in your life, then we need to pray before you read any further:

> Father, I pray as Paul did that "my speech and my preaching was not with enticing words of man's wisdom, but in demonstration of the Spirit and of power, that their faith should not stand in the wisdom of men but in the power of God." (1Cor. 2:4, 5) I also pray that You would give the reader a heart and mind to *receive* the truth in this book, that will enlighten them regarding all that the Word says about "the things that are freely given to us of God." (v.12) Give them a heart of flesh to receive and understand all the benefits of Jesus death and resurrection

over 2000 years ago. Show them the power of Your Word, His Name, and the Blood until they *believe*, and *take* the fullness of their meaning into their hearts, so they can do what You lead them to do *by faith*, with the expectation of *miracles* to follow in Jesus' Name, amen!

Now say: "I am willing to change to a better way. I am willing to *believe the Word—Truth—**Jesus**!*"

If ye be willing and obedient,
ye shall eat the good of the land
—Isaiah 1:19

But whoso looketh into the perfect law of liberty
And continueth therein, he being not a forgetful hearer,
but a doer of the work, this man shall be [blessed] in his deed.
—James 1:25

Chapter 1

Only Believe: God's Love

In this was manifested the love of God toward us,
because that God sent his only begotten Son into the world,
that we might live through him.
Herein is love, not that we loved God, but that he loved us,
and sent his Son to be the propitiation for our sins.
—1 John 4:9,10

And hast loved them, as thou hast loved me.
—John 17:23c

And we have known and believed the
love that God hath to us.
God is love;
and he that dwelleth in love dwelleth in God,
and God in him.
—1 John 4:16

Believe the love, then—take it! Since we are to do all in love
and to love others, *we first have to have love before you can give
it away.* So meditate on God's love for you, beginning at what
Jesus did for you on the cross, and have the same compassion
for others as He had for you, then sow love—give it away.

Jesus said, "By this shall all men know that ye are my
disciples, if ye have love one to another (John 13:35)." "This is

my commandment, That ye love one another, as I have loved you (John 15:12)." Ask God to help you to love others and anoint you to do it. Ask Him to give you ideas, and then obey *the promptings of the Holy Spirit* (John 6:63), because God loves them also. Your love may draw them to Him. Let them see Jesus' love in you.

He shows His love by giving you assurance that He will take care of you and not leave you alone. Therefore, there should be no fear. Verse 18: "But perfect love casteth out fear."

The Amplified verse below makes that abundantly clear.

For He [God] Himself has said, I will not in any way fail you nor give you up nor leave you without support. [I will] not, [I will] not in any degree leave you helpless nor forsake nor let [you] down (relax My hold on you)! [Assuredly not!]
—Hebrews 13:5b

As I was with Moses, so I will be with thee:
I will not fail thee, nor forsake thee.
—Joshua 1:5

When Moses asked to see God's glory, He said He would make all of His *goodness* pass before him, and He proclaimed, "The Lord, the Lord God, merciful and gracious, long-suffering and abundant in goodness and truth, keeping mercy for thousands" (Ex. 34:6).

Micah 7:18: "Because He delighteth in mercy."[2]

---

[2]   Micah 6:8 NKJV, Strong's #2617–mercy: kindness, lovingkindness; unfailing love; tenderness, faithfulness.

1 Chronicles 16:34: "Oh give thanks unto the Lord; for He is good; for his mercy endureth for ever."

Matthew 14:14: "And Jesus went forth, and saw a great multitude, and was moved with compassion[3] toward them, and he healed their sick." Jesus' actions were evidence of God's love for the needy.

Ephesians 2:4, 5, 7 (Amplified):

> But God—so rich is He in His mercy! Because of and in order to satisfy the great and wonderful and intense love with which He loved us, even when we were dead (slain) by [our own] shortcomings and trespasses, He made us alive together in fellowship and in union with Christ; [He gave us the very life of Christ Himself, the same new life with which He quickened Him, for] it is by grace (His favor and mercy which you did not deserve) that you are saved (delivered from judgment and made partakers of Christ's salvation). He did this that He might clearly demonstrate through the ages to come the immeasurable (limitless, surpassing) riches of His free grace (His unmerited favor) in [His] kindness and goodness of heart toward us in Christ Jesus.

Ephesians 3:17–19 (Amplified):

> May you be rooted deep in love and founded securely on love, that you may have the power

---

[3] NKJV, Strong's #4697: To be moved with deep compassion or pity. It is the direct motive for at least five of Jesus' miracles.

and be strong to apprehend and grasp with all the saints [God's devoted people, the experience of that love] what is the breadth and length an height and depth [of it]; [that you may really come] to know [practically, through experience for yourselves] the love of Christ, which far surpasses mere knowledge [without experience].

Here Paul is trying to get you to understand how wonderful the love of God is, and *believe it is for you!* Just like when you love someone, you try to show them by doing things for them: offering to help them to make their life easier, praying for them, surprising them with something they really want, and protecting them from harm. God's love is all this and more, as it says in verse 20, "Able to do exceeding abundantly above all that we ask or think." He is able to bless you in big ways and little ways, to keep you going when things get difficult, because He loves you. <u>Believe the love!</u>

And finally Romans 8:38, 39 (Amplified):

For I am persuaded beyond doubt (am sure) neither death, nor life, nor angels, nor principalities, nor things impending and threatening nor things to come, nor powers, nor height nor depth, nor anything else in all creation will be able to separate us from the love of God which is in Christ Jesus our Lord.

This is why we should not be discouraged or *fearful*. Fear is a door opener to the enemy, but 2 Timothy 1:7 says, "God hath not given us the spirit of fear; but of power, and of love, and of a sound mind." He has given you *power* to overcome it, because of His *love* and a *sound mind*, which is the fruit from that promise. So anytime fearful thoughts come to you (they are not from God), shut and lock the door with this Scripture. Then say it, or as much as you can remember: **"Nothing will separate me from the love of God, which is in Christ Jesus, my Lord!"**

The only way we can know and walk in God's love is to stay in union with Him—the greatest lover. Galatians 5:6b: "But faith which worketh by love." So since God is love, we increase in love and faith by association with Him. When we focus on Jesus, always saying what He would say and doing what He would do, we are learning to 'walk in love' as He did.

So we can see by these Bible references that *God is love*, He is merciful, compassionate, and faithful. As a sign of His mercy, compassion and loving-kindness, people get healed, even if they do nothing, as in Matthew 14:14 and many other verses.

Faith in His love will bring Blessings
—F. F. Bosworth, *Christ the Healer*

Chapter 2

Only Believe: The Word

O the depth of the riches both of the
wisdom and knowledge of God!
How unsearchable are his judgments,
and his ways past finding out!
—Romans 11:33

Believe/belief: to believe, to be persuaded of; to place confidence in, to trust; as a noun: faith. (Vine's) Romans 10:9 NKJV, Strong's #4100: The verb form of *pistis*, faith. It means to trust in, have faith in, be fully convinced of, acknowledge, and rely on. It expresses reliance upon and a personal trust *that produces obedience*. It includes submission and a positive confession of the lordship of Jesus.

I am writing this to *persuade* you to *trust* in, have faith in, until you are *fully convinced, acknowledge,* and *rely on* the Word to receive all that you are believing.

Before we go any further, it's imperative you *believe* the Word. Second Timothy 3:16 NKJV: "All Scripture[4] is given by inspiration of God[5] and is profitable for doctrine, for reproof, for correction, for instruction in righteousness, that the man

---

[4]   *Graphe* points to the divine author with the idea that what is written remains forever identified as the living voice of God. (Jon 5:39 NKJV)

[5]   Footnote: literally means "God-breathed"

of God may be perfect, thoroughly furnished unto all good works." So the Bible is our workbook to give us all the help we need to live this life.

Only Believe! is also a workbook, like the Bible. Just reading it will not change your circumstances. It works when you work it and *do what it says!*

As I shared in the introduction about Proverbs 4:22, let's look at verses: 20–24 more closely:

> *Command*: My son, attend to my words;
>> incline thine ear unto my sayings.
> Let them not depart from thine eyes;
>> keep them in the midst of thine heart.
> *Benefit*: For they are life unto those that find them,
>> and health to all their flesh.
> *Command*: Keep thy heart with all diligence;
> *Benefit*: for out of it are the issues of life.
> *Command*: Put away from thee a froward mouth,
>> and perverse lips put far from thee.

Attend means to look after. *Diligence* means the constant effort to accomplish what is undertaken. *Froward* means habitually disposed to disobedience and opposition or adverse. Briefly the synonym of *perverse* is corrupt . . . improper . . . incorrect.[6]

From this Proverb, Solomon makes it quite clear to *attend/look after* the reading of Scriptures, keeping them before our eyes and in our hearts *with constant effort*, because there is a benefit of life and health to all our flesh. Then he says to put

---

[6]   Merriam-Webster Inc

away from you a difficult to control and corrupt mouth, which is speaking without thinking or spewing foolish and coarse words, you may regret later.

This sounds like strong counsel from the Lord, because His rules guide, protect, *provide,* and bless those that put them into practice. John 14:15 says, "If you love me, keep my commandments." The MSG says, "If you love me, show it by doing what I have told you."

Obey Proverbs 4:20–22

One day I was watching a ministry I had recorded,
and the minister said he had gotten a
cold or the flu the previous fall.
He did everything he knew to do, but continued
to feel good and bad day after day.
So he asked the Lord, "Where am I missing it?" and He said
"The memory of a baked potato doesn't give
any enjoyment or nourishment."
Then He reminded him of the Scripture Proverbs 4:20–22.
Once he began reading Scriptures on
healing, he got well and stayed well.
* * *

Since Solomon was the wisest man of that time, when he asked God to give him wisdom ("a wise and understanding heart" 1Kings 3:12) to rule His people, we can assume that this is what God wants us to do also.

Romans 15:4: "For whatever things were written aforetime were written [for our learning], that we through the patience and comfort of the Scriptures might [have hope]." That means your neck is outstretched expecting *to see* what you are *hoping for.*

> If we hope for what we do not see,
> we eagerly wait for *it* with perseverance.
> —Romans 8:25

Next we need to *believe* John 1:1AB, re: The Word—"In the beginning [before all time] was the Word (Christ), and the Word was with God, and the Word was God Himself." Verse 14: "And the Word (Christ) became flesh (human, incarnate) and tabernacle (fixed His tent of flesh, lived awhile) among us, and we [actually] saw His glory (His honor, His majesty), such glory as an only begotten son receives from his father, full of grace (favor, lovingkindness) and truth." (Also see 1 John 1:1-3)

> Who being the brightness of His glory,
> and the express image of His person,
> and upholding all things by the Word of his power.
> —Hebrews 1:3

The Word is Jesus: Wonderful, Counselor, Mighty God, Prince of Peace, Everlasting Father, King of Kings and Lord of Lords, and so much more. (Isa. 9:6; Rev 19:16) So when you read the Word, you are spending time with Jesus. "Jesus became the physical embodiment of the Word of God."—Jack Hayford (see contributors) The more you read it, the more you get *the mind of Christ*—how He thinks.

Nowhere in the Bible does Jesus say: I'm hungry, I'm cold, hot, feel like I'm catching a cold, my back aches, that guy offended me, or I just can't forgive them. He said what he heard his father say, and won great victories by saying: "It is written" (Matt. 4:4, 7, 10), because he believed what was written. He is our example!

Jesus said in John 10:30, "I and My Father are one." He also said to Philip, "He that hath seen Me has seen the Father" (John 14:9b). And in John 8:58 NKJV, "Verily, verily, I say unto you, Before Abraham was, I AM."

Remember Jesus said to know the truth and the truth will set you free. The Truth makes you free from the facts (what you can see or what you've been told), for what can be seen can be changed—it's temporal. (2 Cor. 4:17, 18) So we need to read the Truth (the Bible) everyday, and books by writers anointed with the Holy Spirit, because "the word of God is quick and powerful" (Heb. 4:12). Isn't that an accurate description of Jesus from the Bible? Think about Him stilling the storm with His words "Peace, be still"; and casting out the demons from the man that was filled with them. Or, going into the temple area and driving out the moneychangers with a whip. (Mark 4:39; 5:1-9; 11:15)

For thou has magnified thy Word above all thy Name.
—Psalms 138:2b

Hebrews 1:3 AB: when describing Jesus, "He is the perfect imprint and very image of [God's] nature, upholding and maintaining and guiding and propelling the universe by His mighty Word of power." Shouldn't we use that *mighty Word of power* to change things in our lives, as He turned the darkness into light, and when He spoke words of faith in the beginning to create all things, since *we were created in His image?* (Gen.1:2, 3, 27)

Deuteronomy 6:4–9:

> Hear, O Israel: The Lord our God is one Lord: and thou shalt love the Lord thy God with all thine heart, and with all thy soul, and with all thy might. And these words, which I command thee this day, shall be in thine heart: and thou shalt teach them diligently unto thy children, and shalt talk of them when thou sittest in thine house, and when thou walkest by the way, and when thou liest down, and when thou risest up. And thou shalt bind them for a sign upon thine hand, and they shall be as frontlets between thine eyes. And thou shalt write them upon the posts of thy house, and on the gates.

> But blessed are your eyes, for they see:
> and your ears, for they hear.
> —Matthew 13:16

So we are commanded to keep the Word in front of our eyes, and use it in every part of our lives. Colossians 3:16: "Let the word of Christ dwell in you richly in all wisdom;" and Jesus said: "For unto every one that hath shall be given, and he shall have abundance: but from him that hath not shall be taken away even that which he hath" (Matt. 25:29).

Since every Word of God is for our teaching, if we applied this to the amount of Word we get into our hearts daily, then we will have abundance for the difficult times to sustain us. But if we know a little of the Word, we will lose it or be robbed of it by the enemy. If you are not going forward up a hill, you will automatically fall back. We must keep going forward with all the help we can get from Jesus, our Sustainer.

> * Know the Word so well, that it will be the first thing you will think (your reflex action) to discern between the Truth and error: the lies and deception of the devil.

> * Know it so well you will be able *to stand on it* no matter what things look like, feel like or seem like, even when nothing is happening, till you can praise the Lord in faith.

You need to be *fully persuaded*, so that out of the abundance of your heart your mouth speaks with confidence. (Matt.12:34b) Remember, no giant: physically, financially, relationally is too difficult for God Almighty! The Red Sea, a giant, the violent King Saul, the walls of Jericho, the wicked King Manasseh, Jezebel, an army of thousands, and plagues were all conquered and put in their place.

> As for God, His way is perfect:
> the word of the Lord is tried:
> He is buckler to all those that trust in Him.
> —Psalms 18:30

What to Do Next:

Begin now! Redeem the time you have lost. "Redeeming the time, because the days are evil" (Eph. 5:16). There is a commercial that says: "Life comes at you fast!" Then there is a scene of a couple driving off the road, destroying their vehicle. My advice: <u>be prepared</u>, "because your adversary the devil walks about like a roaring lion, seeking whom he may devour" (1 Peter 5:8 NKJV). Don't let it be you!

Make reading the Word daily "top priority" in your life. It should be the first thing you do each day when you get up. God is a jealous god, so anything else you do before spending time with Him, puts Him in second place, which dishonors Him. "Keep yourselves from idols." Any god, object, or pursuit other than that directed by God's revealed will and way declared in His Son is an idol. (1John 5:20, 21 NKJV footnote) Be careful about how much time you spend on the Internet each day; it can become an idol.

Even when you go on vacation or are very busy, *don't eliminate reading the Word*—spending time with the Lord. The devil doesn't go on vacation, but he hopes you will cut out this important time. This habit of daily reading your Bible is like when you quit exercising or taking supplements, all the benefits stop—you're back to zero!

"But without faith it is impossible to please him: for he that cometh to God must believe that he is, and that he is a rewarder of them that diligently seek him" (Heb.11:6). So there is a reward for diligently seeking Him as you read the Word, and finding out what He has for you that day. It is the best way to get to *know Him* and *believe* in Him. It also develops your faith, and you will never regret it!

Once you have done these things and are convinced that the Word is truth, <u>agree with it!</u> Agree with God Who loves you. Agree with Him as if you were standing in front of Him and shaking His hand, because you have accepted His wisdom through the Word you have read, which should *settle it forever*! Claim your rights to the promises of God, because they belong to Believers!

> The fear of the Lord is the beginning of wisdom:
> and the knowledge of the Holy One is understanding.
> —Proverbs 9:10

Before Moses died, he laid hands on Joshua, who had been Moses right-hand man for years, to take over the leadership of His people. Then God spoke to Joshua: "This book of the law shall not depart out thy mouth; but thou shalt mediate therein day and night, that thou mayest observe to do according to all that is written therein: for then thou shalt make thy way prosperous, and then thou shalt have good success" (Josh. 1:8). So He is saying: Be consistent!

We are not under the Law, but under Grace and have a better covenant through "the Blood of Jesus Christ." So shouldn't we have more success by reading about the New Covenant, which Jesus purchased for us as described in the New Testament? (Heb.8:6; 13:20)

So if God commanded, not suggested, that the leader of His people needed to know His ways daily (and do all that was written), to be prosperous and successful, don't you think we should also take this advice? Here is another Scripture with a reward for our obedience to do what He says. Of course, it is dependent on whether you want to go *the easy way* with God's help, or go the hard way (your own) without it! Did you know that if you don't obey God's Word, that you're rejecting it? So a good confession would be: "**I choose God's ways.**"

> If they obey and serve him,
> they shall spend their days in prosperity,
> and their years in pleasures.
> —Job 36:11

Be teachable to receive anything from the Lord, especially healing. "For this people's heart is waxed gross, and their ears are dull of hearing, and their eyes they have closed; lest at any time they should see with their eyes, and hear with their ears, and should understand with their heart, and should be converted, and I should heal them" (Matt. 13:15). So open your eyes to see, ears to hear, and hearts to understand, that way you get a triple impact into your life of all that God has promised you in His Word. *Accept the Truth and make it your own!*

Renew your mind. Don't allow your mind to go where it wants to. If idle hands are the devil's workshop, than an idle mind is his playground. Don't give it to him. Put on the whole armor of God by girding your loins with truth—the Word. Memorize Eph. 6:11–18, or see it in *Only Believe: You Have Authority* for how I do it.

If you don't read the Word, you won't know what belongs to you, what can help you, or what to say to change your body *or* circumstances.

It is written, That man shall not live by bread alone,
but by every word of God.
—Luke 4:4

Read, listen to, or watch everything the Bible says regarding the subject of healing, or your need. Read devotionals by Spirit-filled leaders with fruit in their lives, who will help to give you understanding of the things happening in your life. Then go over it over and over again. Create your own seminar by doing nothing else for one day to a week, depending upon your symptoms or circumstances. If you can get away to "a solitary place", where you have no other responsibilities, do it! Keep focused until you are full of the Word regarding your need. Saturate yourself with it. You are worth it!

Blessed are they that hear the word of God, and keep it.
—Luke 11: 28

The Word Heals MS

There is a testimony of a woman with multiple sclerosis,
who went to hear Mark Brazee* at a
small campmeeting at her church.
She shared that she suffered with the disease for a long time
and couldn't even walk without crutches.
She had been doing all she knew to do,
but when she heard she needed to
saturate herself with God's Word on healing,
she spent the afternoon studying for hours,
until so much faith rose up inside her

> *that she wrote in her Bible "Healed by*
> *the power of God!" and dated it.*
> *She said she knew in her heart that things*
> *were going to change that night.*
> *So when she came back to get prayed for by the Evangelist,*
> *who laid hands on her, she was instantly healed!*

*Author of *365 Days of Healing*, Harrison
House* 1999; used by permission
* * *

Use your time wisely confessing the Word, praising God, singing songs, listening to teaching and *relistening*, while you are walking, driving, showering, making meals, shopping, exercising, mowing the lawn or anything else. Don't be concerned about others; you'll probably never see them again. Besides, people talk to themselves all the time. *Make your talking productive* to cause good fruit in your life.

1 Peter 1:13 (Amplified):

> So brace up your minds; be sober (circumspect, morally alert); set your hope wholly and unchangeably on the grace (divine favor) that is coming to you when Jesus Christ is revealed. Verse18–21: You must know (recognize) that you were redeemed from the useless way of living inherited by tradition from [your] forefathers, not with corruptible things [such as] silver and gold, but [you were purchased] with the precious blood of Christ,(the Messiah), like that of a [sacrificial] lamb without

blemish or spot. It is true that He was chosen before the foundation of the world, but He was brought out to public view in these last days for the sake of you. Through Him you believe (adhere to, rely on) God, Who raised Him up from the dead and gave Him honor and glory, so that your faith and hope are [centered and rest] in God.

> Blessed is the man that trusteth in the Lord,
> and whose hope the Lord is.
> —Jeremiah 17:7

* * *

We recently recorded and watched the old musical drama *Carousel* with Shirley Jones and Gordon McRae. Even though there were many songs that became popular from the movie, the story line led you to believe that no matter how you lived your life, you would go to Heaven, which does not agree with the Word.

It began in a 'star land' where Billy Bigalow told the head man about his life before he arrived there, attempting to *lie* in the process. He had married Julie, an innocent, gullible, infatuated-with-him-young lady, who worked at the garment factory, but let him know she was in love with him. This was before he lost his job as the carousel barker, because *he refused to submit to authority* and *wanted to do things his own way.*

> For rebellion is as the sin of witchcraft,
> and stubbornness is as iniquity and idolatry.
> —1 Sam. 15:23a

This happened the same night that her boss *happened* to stop by where she was meeting Billy with her friend, and offer to walk her home, as it was late and she had a curfew, but *she refused*—second bad decision. After they got married they moved in with her aunt, but Billy still *couldn't find a job that suited him.* So a conniving friend suggested they steal the payroll from Julie's former boss, and only *threaten him* with a knife to get it.

The "friend", Jigger, egged Billy on until the night they attempted the robbery, but the boss was prepared for an attack, and Billy ended up getting stabbed with his own knife when he fell on it. So he left his grieving pregnant wife, who loved him and ended up in Heaven??? Nowhere in the movie did Billy show any evidence that he was a Christian, except for the conversation with Jigger, about how they would be judged someday. He had no faith or hope trusting in God.

The reason I shared this movie is because most movies lead you to believe you are going to Heaven no matter how you have lived, which is a lie from the devil. To set things straight, the only people in Heaven will be those whose names are written in the Lamb's book of life. "And there shall in no wise enter into it any thing that defileth, neither whatsoever worketh abomination, or maketh a lie: but they which are written in the Lamb's book of life" (Rev. 21:27).

First Corinthians 6:9,10 NKJV also makes it clear: "Do you not know that the unrighteous will not inherit the kingdom of God? Do be not deceived. Neither fornicators, nor idolaters, nor adulterers, nor homosexuals, nor sodomites, nor thieves, nor covetous, nor drunkards, nor revilers, nor extortioners will inherit the kingdom of God." Notice some of these sinful actions affect the person, while the others abuse people or rob them of their rights in some way. They are definitely not Christ-like!

You see we are not *saved* just to get a ticket to Heaven, but to do "good works" here on earth: to promote the Gospel, train disciples and *be a blessing to others.* These are signs of a transformed life. Jesus said greater works would we do because He was going back to His father. (John 14:12) There is no way we can do greater works than Jesus, without being trained in "the keys of the kingdom" (Matt.16:19), so we can walk in *great faith* as He did.

> This is a faithful saying,
> and these things I will that thou affirm constantly,
> that they which have believed in God might
> be careful to maintain good works.
> These things are good and profitable unto men.
> —Titus 3:8

James 2:26: "For as the body without the Spirit is dead, so faith without works is dead also." That could mean the physical body, or it could mean the body of Christ—the church. (1 Cor. 12:27) We know at death the spirit of a person that is a Believer lives on and will go to Heaven—"Absent from the body, and to be present with the Lord" (2 Cor.5:8). But the lost person's spirit will spend eternity in hell, because he refused *the free gift of eternal life through Jesus Christ.* A church without the Spirit is dead, and filled with people who religiously follow its rules of doctrine. They don't want to or are afraid to step out of their comfort zone to share the Gospel, because it requires faith and obedience, besides *a love for others!*

The Bible says we can't do anything without Christ, and, I might add, it can get you into a lot of trouble; but if you "Walk in the Spirit, ye shall not fulfill the lust of the flesh" (Gal. 5:16) —you won't do what you want to do. You'll ask the Lord and follow His leading, but this takes practice, practice, and more practice. It requires *yielding your whole self over to the* Lord Jesus Christ. Another way to say it is dying to selfishness— self-centeredness, which is satan's character.

Let Jesus be Lord of your life!

To begin, we need to submit ourselves to God *by faith* through Jesus Christ for forgiveness of sins, and eternal life, because "As it is written, there is none righteous, no not one" (Rom. 3:10). "For all have sinned, and come short of the glory of God." (v. 23)

I never understood how a baby could be called a sinner until our pastor amplified what this meant. You know that shortly after a baby is born they begin demanding to be fed, changed, etc. immediately! If they don't get what they want, they get angry and cry louder and longer. Then as they grow a little that changes to temper tantrums.

After that when they do something wrong (so they won't be punished), they may tell a lie about what happened. When they get old enough they may argue with you, and not do what you've told them to do. Now can you imagine Jesus doing any of this as a baby, a toddler, a child or a teen? No, He was blameless!

"But God commendeth his love toward us, in that, while we were yet sinners, Christ died for us . . . Wherefore, as by one man sin entered into the world, and death by sin; and so death passed upon all men, for that all have sinned" (Rom. 5:8, 12).

"For the wages of sin is death; but [the gift of God] is eternal life through Jesus Christ our Lord" (Rom. 6:23).

"For God so loved the world that He gave His only begotten Son, that whosoever believeth in Him should not perish but have everlasting life" (John 3:16).

"That if you confess with your mouth the Lord Jesus and believe in your heart that God has raised Him from the dead, you will be saved. For with the heart one believes unto righteousness, and with the mouth confession is made unto salvation. For the scripture saith, whosoever believeth on him shall not be ashamed. For whosoever shall call upon the name of the Lord shall be saved" (Rom.10:9–11, 13 NKJV).

This is the day of Salvation!

Neither is there salvation in any other:
for there is none other name under heaven given among men,
whereby we must be saved.
—Acts 4:12

After Peter was baptized with the Holy Spirit, he spoke boldly to the rulers and elders of Israel, which caused them to marvel. "And they realized that they had been with Jesus" (Acts 4:13a NKJV). So he is saying no other name of a prophet, god, leader, priest, Pope, Buddha, Mohamed, or others can guarantee a future home in Heaven.

And this is life eternal,
that they might know thee the only true God,
and Jesus Christ, whom thou hast sent.
—John 17:3

Also: "Jesus answered and said unto them, This is the work of God, that ye believe on him whom He hath sent" (John 6:29).

Salvation is more than a ticket to Heaven. It is soundness, prosperity, deliverance, preservation, happiness, and general well-being. It is an all-inclusive word signifying forgiveness, healing, safety, liberation and restoration. Christ's salvation is total in scope for the total man: spirit, soul, and body. (Acts 28:28 NKJV, Strong's #4992) Why wouldn't anyone want so great a Salvation?

Proverbs 3:5, 6: "Trust in the LORD with all thine heart; and lean not unto thine own understanding. In all thy ways acknowledge Him, and He shall direct thy paths." The reward is the leading of the Holy Spirit in all you do, which will be according to *His will and love for you*, not to harm you. This happens when you receive Him as Lord of your life; He gives you a part of Himself: the Holy Spirit, the Counselor, because Hebrews 13: 5 says, "I will never leave thee, nor forsake thee."

So you need to *believe* and *confess the Word* in order to be saved from death, or what ever unpleasant circumstances you are in: sickness, debt, lack, loneliness, confusion, family problems, etc. Remember in order to be saved, we need to *say* or *confess* something we believe. In this case acknowledging that *Jesus is Lord,* invites His presence and power to rule in your life and circumstances.

Recapping: Today I offered you a ticket to Heaven *free!* I hope you accepted it <u>by faith</u>, so the Holy Spirit can cancel the sin and sickness in your life, and set you on the path to Heaven. Did you know that? Angels are also available to you upon request. (Heb.1:14) Did you know about this benefit? But it's your responsibility to stay on that path by following the instructions in the Bible.

God knew you'd never get to Heaven the way you were, so He offers you a new start, canceling all the sins of your past, up to the moment you accept Him *by grace through faith.* (Eph. 2:8) Part of His requirements is repenting of the wrong things you've done, which means turning *away from them.* It's like what Jesus said to the woman caught in adultery: "Go and sin no more" (John 8:11).

> Beloved, if our heart condemn us not,
> then have we confidence toward God.
> —1 John 3:21

If we don't change here on earth, Heaven will be like hell, because of all the unchanged liars, killers, thieves, sexually immoral, idolaters, etc. (1 Cor. 6:9, 10) God has a perfect, peaceful, beautiful kingdom awaiting His children without sorrow, disease, pain, or any other curse called Heaven, and He doesn't want it contaminated.

When Jesus is Lord of your life, it's like a king that fights for His people, protects them, sets the law, judges the situations, provides for their needs, requires a tax (tithe) and expects honor. Matthew 7:21 says, "Not everyone who saith unto Me, Lord, Lord, shall enter into the kingdom of heaven, but he that doeth the will of My Father which is in heaven."

So when you make Jesus the Lord of your life, you are submitting to Him and allowing Him to be in charge of you. Remember He is a loving Lord, Who only wants the best for you, so you need not fear obedience to Him. Trust Him completely and He will not fail you, and He has even promised to give you the desires of your heart. (Ps. 37:4)

And whatsoever we ask, we receive of him,
because we keep his commandments,
and *do those things that are pleasing in his sight.*
—1 John 3:22 (Emphasis added)

You can show your love and appreciation for Him by reading His Word regularly, and obeying it, which is serving Him. How else are you going to show the One Who loves you so much, that He came to suffer for you, and deliver you from the lake of fire?

And that He died for all,
that they which live should not . . . live unto themselves,
but unto Him which died for them, and rose again.
—2 Corinthians 5:15

Try to answer these honestly: Is Jesus lord over your schedule, your leisure time, your body, your mind, your money? Or do you keep Him in a box just for Sundays? Is He lord over your family? Do you trust Him to take care of them when you pray and *believe* He will?

Do you know the love of God enough to be able to say "I surrender all"?

I hope I have caused you to really think about this, and what you would answer: "Why should I let you into Heaven?"

For whosoever shall call upon the Name of the Lord
shall be saved.
—Romans 10:13

Repent therefore and be converted,
that your sins may be blotted out,
*so that times of refreshing may come
from the presence of the Lord.*
—Acts 3:19 NKJV (Emphasis added)

If not, pray this prayer *from your heart*:

God, in Heaven, I *believe Jesus is Your Son,* Who died on the cross and was raised from the dead, as Substitute for my sins and sicknesses. Forgive my complacency, and my denying You time in my life. I *repent* of anything I've said, thought or done wrong up to this moment. *I believe* as You have forgiven me, I also forgive myself and all others in my life. **Jesus**, come into my heart, and live in me and through me. **I receive You now as my Lord and Savior.** I take all that You bought and paid for me on the cross. I *believe* you have heard me, and I expect to be a new person with the help of the Holy Spirit to counsel me in all my ways, amen.

"Blessed is he whose transgression is forgiven, whose sin is covered. Blessed is the man to whom the Lord does not impute iniquity, and in whose spirit there is no deceit" (Ps. 32:1, 2 NKJV).

"As far as the east is from the west, so far hath he removed or transgressions from us" (Ps. 103:12).

"But as many as received him, to them gave he power to become the sons of God, even to them that believe on his name" (John 1:12).

"He that believeth on the Son hath everlasting life: and he that believeth not the Son shall not see life; but the wrath of God abideth on him" (John 3:36).

"He that believeth and is baptized shall be saved; but he that believeth not shall be damned" (Mark 16:16).

Baptism is the public declaration of your belief that you have accepted *Jesus as your Savior and Lord.* It also says that you have been "born again" into a new life. Your past has been buried with Christ, and you've been given a new heart. So don't put it off; contact your pastor or the new *Bible believing* church you will be going to regularly, and get water baptized.

Chapter 3

Only Believe: The Holy Spirit

"The Holy Spirit is the divine agent in
revealing God's heart and will."
—Alexander Maclaren

Being filled with the Holy Spirit is a daily benefit, and *a
necessity* to accomplish all things, besides *getting you through
difficulties.* The Holy Spirit is the third Person of the Trinity,
and helps us hear from God, among other important things.
Jesus said in John 14:26 NKJV, "But the Helper, the Holy Spirit,
whom the Father will send in My name, He will teach you all
things and bring to your remembrance all things that I said to
you." Hearing from the Helper (Comforter) is vital to your well
being. He is our Wonderful Counselor!

The Spirit of Counsel is Someone Who knows everything
about every matter, and gives us that counsel, if we are open to
his promptings, to deal wisely in every affair of life—He is in
the Believer. In Job 12:13 the verse says, "With him is *wisdom*
and *strength*, he hath *counsel* and *understanding.*" (Emphasis
added) Notice this is four of the seven Spirits of God mentioned
in Isaiah 11:2 referring to Jesus, the Branch, and they are all
provided by the Holy Spirit, so we can live in this world in a
better way every day.

First Corinthians 2:7–10: "Eye hath not seen, nor ear heard,
neither have entered into the heart of man, the things which God

hath prepared for them who love Him. But God hath revealed them unto us by His Spirit." Notice that the *revelation comes to those that love God*, which means they have a personal relationship with Him. They spend time with Him. That means they read the Bible regularly, and talk to the Lord about their daily concerns; besides thanking Him for all that He does in their life—that's giving Him glory. He should also get glory when we are blessed, healed and prosperous or not!

Benefits of the Holy Spirit:

Teacher—reveals truth
Reminder—of the promises
Counselor—shows the way
Enabler—strengthens
Power—to accomplish
Comforter—brings peace

I appreciate everything: hot water, sunshine, dry roads in winter, a bed to sleep in, food in the refrigerator, clothes in the closet, steady income, etc., etc. There are millions of people that do not have what most people take for granted. Once again *we should be praising God continually!* He lives in the praises of His people. (Ps 22:3) So the more we praise Him, the more we keep our relationship alive to hear from Him. Wouldn't you spend time with someone who enjoys your company?

Just think about it, if you never hear from a loved one, how do you know they care? If someone really cares, they will make an effort to keep in touch with you. Since **God is love**, He is always reaching out to us, because *He cares for us*. The Bible says, "Thou shalt love the Lord thy God with all thy heart, and with all thy soul, and with all thy mind." The MSG: "Love the Lord your God with all your passion and prayer and intelligence" (Matt. 22:37). Totally committed.

Just imagine how your life would have been if your parents, teachers, employers, neighbors, state representatives, judges, government officials, movie and television producers did this! Our lives would be blessed! There wouldn't be the lying, selfishness, and greed in our world. That's why we have to do what 1Timothy 2:1, 2 says and pray with all manner of prayer "for all men; for kings, and for all that are in authority, that we my lead a quiet and peaceable life in all godliness and reverence." NJKV

<u>Praying in the Spirit</u> is extremely helpful, especially when we don't know what else to do. It is also part of the armor of God instructions in Ephesians 6:18, "praying always with all prayer and supplication in the Spirit, and watching thereunto with all perseverance and supplication for all saints."

> Now if anyone does not have the Spirit of Christ,
> he is not His.
> —Romans 8:9 NKJV

How do you pray "in the Spirit" without being *Spirit-filled*? You can't. In fact it is very difficult to pray very long with your mind, which is limited, but the Holy Spirit knows everything— He is the third person of the Trinity after all! So He knows what needs to be prayed to change the situation, and God has given us His Spirit to do the praying. So we have no excuse if things go wrong, because He has provided a *Person* to help us. In fact, Jude 20 tells us to *build yourselves up* "on your most holy faith by praying in the Holy Ghost", which makes our weak prayers effective.

It is like connecting your I-phone into the recharge outlet, or any other device, such as an MP3 player into the computer, to get the wisdom, strength, and faith to do what He has called you to do *with ease*. We increase by association—connection. Just like you see the tiny connection symbol moving across the screen as it recharges it, we get built up when we pray in the Spirit.

If you asked someone for the way to get to a particular destination and he told you, then when you followed his instructions, you would arrive there. If a doctor told you to take a prescription three times a day, and you would be healed, why wouldn't you *believe God* and do what He says, when He has given you *all you need in His love* to be healed, blessed, restored, enabled and prospered?

Jesus said, "If ye then, being evil, know how to give good gifts unto your children, how much more shall your heavenly Father give the Holy Spirit to them who ask Him!" (Luke 11:13). So ask Him and **receive the Holy Spirit**, then begin by saying hallelujah, hallelujah, hallelujah, hallelujah, praise the Lord, hallelujah! Just like the disciples did when they received the baptism of the Holy Spirit in Acts 2:11: they praised God and His wonderful works.

Do like the cast did at the end of the old musical *Hit the Deck* and "Sing Hallelujah". This was after the three Navy men got their girls and everything had been straightened out that had been chaos. The final scene is *everyone* on deck singing and waving their hands in the air: "Hallelujah, hallelujah and you'll shoo the blues away. Hallelujah, hallelujah will get you through the darkest day. Satan lies awatin' and creating skies of grey. Sing hallelujah, hallelujah it helps to shoo the clouds away. When cares pursue yah, sing hallelujah and you'll shoo the blues away."

Blessed with Power!

In the church where I was raised, I had
never heard of the Holy Spirit
accept the annual mention of Pentecost on
the Christian calendar in the spring,
(which I never remembered or understood, because
I was blinded about this by the enemy), until my
Spirit-filled friend asked me if I wanted it.
So I said "If it's good, I want it."
Then I asked and <u>believed</u> *I received*
"the baptism of the Holy Spirit",
as she prayed for me and guided me;
but the evidence came a few days later,
when I was doing the laundry
in the basement of our old house, and praising God.
Suddenly prayer language started bubbling
up from my inner most being! Wow!
That was exciting! I was praising, cry-
ing and rejoicing all at the same time!
What a tremendous blessing and life
changing experience for me!

* * *

The disciples didn't know it was going to happen, but Jesus breathed on them and said to them, **Receive the Holy Spirit**. (John 20:22) And in Acts 1:4, 5: "And, being assembled together with them, commanded them that they should not depart from Jerusalem, but wait for the promise of the Father, which, saith he, ye have heard of me. For John truly baptized with water: but ye shall be baptized with the Holy Ghost not many days hence." Verse 8: "**But ye shall receive power, after that the Holy Ghost is come upon you**." And then He was taken up. So the last thing He wanted them to remember was that *the Holy Spirit was coming to empower them* to be witnesses everywhere, which He did!

He came in a mighty way that first time (Acts 2:2–4), and caused the words of the disciples to change to "other tongues", or languages of the nations that were there at the time. Then He caused the nations to hear their own languages.

Since He is the same yesterday, today and forever (Heb. 13:8), He can cause your words to change, give you understanding of them, give you confirmation of what He is saying to you, <u>or</u> what you are saying. As it says in John 16:13: "Howbeit when He, the Spirit of truth, is come, he will guide you into all truth: for he shall not speak of himself; but whatsoever he shall hear, that shall he speak: and he will shew you things to come." Isn't that wonderful! What a loving Heavenly Father and Prince of Peace.

Almighty God has provided a way to contact us through the Holy Spirit with tongues or touch, which will confirm He is with us, approving of what we are doing, or promising us the things that are to come. He said He will not leave us orphans, but will come to us in the form of the Holy Spirit. (John 14:18)

So if Jesus can heal bodies with His touch, and there is no distance with Spirit, why can't He touch your body, to let you know He is present? He loves you, is guiding you, or saying "Yes, I agree with that." with goose pimples, an inward shower, a shake, a jerk or maybe a quickening of some other kind. When that happens, respond "What Lord? What do you want me to see or know?" Then when you know, act on what He told you.

If you are obedient to do your part, the Holy Spirit will do His part. It should agree with the Word of God in some way, because He is not going to tell you something that will harm you. Believe His love!

Read the book of Acts and see how He empowered the Believers. Since Paul said to pray "always with all prayer and supplication in the Spirit", could it be possible that He and Silas may have been doing that when a great earthquake shook the prison, and the doors opened? (Acts 16:25, 26) Because it is "Not by might, nor by power, but by the My Spirit saith the Lord of hosts" (Zech. 4:6b).

Holy Spirit Healed Heart

From Joseph Prince's 'Daily Grace Inspirations',
he shared that after he had taught on 1 Corinthians 14:4,
He who speaks in a tongue "edifies himself",
(builds up his spirit, soul and body),
which was confirmed by the brain specialists
at O R U Hospital saying,
that when a person prays in tongues,
his brain releases two chemicals
that are directed to his immune system,
giving it a 35-40% boost.

So one of Pr. Princes' church members
(a seventy-four year old man),
decided to build up his immune system,
when Pr. Prince told everyone
who wanted to be healed of heart problems to stand up.
(He was scheduled for a heart-related
operation, because of a 70% blockage
in two of his arteries and five smaller vessels 80% blocked.)
At the moment he responded by placing
his hand over his heart and
began praying in tongues, the Holy Spirit touched him and
he became a different person.
When he went for his medical checkup,
his surgeon discovered that
his blockages were gone—he literally had a change of heart!
Pray up Your Immune System, (Used by permission)

* * *

Jesus sent the Holy Spirit to help each one of us. We need all the perfect help we can get! So follow the faintest leading of the Holy Spirit—that "still small voice" from inside. (1 Kings 19:12) Sometimes you can waste a lot of time and embarrassment not obeying it. It might be: Don't forget to take an umbrella. Did you remember your checkbook? Do you have the receipt? Call first to be sure they are there, leave early, etc.

One of the most important times you don't want to miss the Holy Spirit's leading is when he begins preparing you for Jesus return to the earth: the Rapture or the "catching away". First

Thessalonians 4:13–18: "For the Lord Himself shall descend from heaven with a shout, with the voice of an archangel, and with the trump of God: and the dead in Christ will rise first. Then we which are alive and remain shall be [caught up] together with them in the clouds, to meet the Lord in the air: and so shall we ever be with the Lord." [It is said that we are that generation that will be a part of this. I believe it!]

If you miss the leading of the Holy Spirit, you could miss *the opportunity*, which causes delays, and extra expense, like when you miss your flight by not being on time; or not buying something when you saw it. Then you have to waste your time and gas searching for it, and probably not getting what you really wanted. [Been there, done that!]

If we had missed the timing of building our new house, we would have missed many blessings, including a $6,000 check our government offered *at that time*, because we were upgrading in our move.

We need to continually be taught by anointed preachers and servants of the Lord on Faith, Healing, Prayer, Provision, Protection, Communion, Exercising Authority, etc. Some of the testimonies and stories that they have told have been unforgettable, and have fit so many situations that I've been able to share with others to *encourage* them.

If you haven't been, begin writing down everything that the Holy Spirit quickens to your spirit. Those words are a *prophecy* to you of what is to come—it is a promise, which gives you hope. Reread those promises frequently to keep up your hope, and then *hang on to them* tenaciously in faith until they come to pass! **If God said it, BELIEVE it!** He is a God that does not lie. (Titus 1:2)

In Ezekiel 36:7 NKJV, He says: "I have raised My hand in an oath." When He promises in the Old Testament, He has said many times then you will know that I am the Lord. (Ex. 6:7) Hebrews 10:23b says: "For He is faithful that promised." So when He says it in at least three places in the Bible that He will do what He says He will do, we can expect Him to keep His word to us also.

He is love! And He hastens to perform His Word—it is living and powerful. (Heb. 4:12) His ways are perfect. Second Peter 1:2: "Grace and peace be multiplied unto you through the knowledge of God, and of Jesus our Lord." So the more we learn about God, we'll be able to receive more of the precious gifts of Grace and peace. The more we read of His mighty acts, the more grace and peace we will have in our circumstances, because "God is no respecter of persons" (Acts 10:34a).

> Oh how great is Thy goodness, which thou
> hast laid up for them that fear thee; which thou
> hast wrought for them that trust in thee before
> the sons of men! . . . O Love the Lord, all ye his
> saints: for the Lord preserveth the faithful, and
> plentifully rewardeth the proud doer. Be of good
> courage, and he shall strengthen your heart, all
> ye that hope in the Lord.
> —Psalms 31: 19, 23, 24

Then lean on, trust in and rely on Him to fulfill those promises. You must <u>believe</u> (no matter what you see or feel) you have heard from Him. **Believe utterly!** See it happening in your imagination; *praising God* while you wait for your manifestation of deliverance or healing.

Vision Restored

*Pastor Joseph Prince of Joseph Prince
Ministries shared a story,
about a blind lady that was led to a great
healing Evangelist for prayer.
He prayed for her and asked her "Now tell me what you see."
She opened her eyes only to be told, "Close your eyes."
Tell me what you see." She opened her
eyes again only to be told,
"I didn't say to open your eyes. I asked you what you saw.
Close your eyes! Now tell me what you see."
This went on until the lady realized
the Evangelist was asking her
what she saw <u>on the inside</u>. Then she
said, "I see myself with sight."
So the Evangelist told her to slowly open her eyes,
and at that moment she opened her eyes to perfect vision!*

The Power in the Seed to Prosper, CD,
May 5, 2002 (Used by permission)

* * *

The lesson is to start seeing yourself with the answer
NOW—*imagine it!* God gave us imagination for good, not evil.
<u>See</u> your answer in what Jesus did for you on the cross. *See
that infirmity on Jesus* (your Substitute), the Lamb of God on
the cross, bearing it for you, which He did! Just like you see

the deleted email being thrown into the trash bin, see your symptoms and *cares cast on* Jesus when He took them Good Friday. Say: "Quicken me Lord, according to *all* Your Word says belongs to me through the cross."

Do you realize Good Friday is the most important *holy day* of the year! It is the day Jesus *took on Himself all the sins of the world, besides all their weaknesses, infirmities and "diseases"*. The Old Testament law said the blood paid for the sins of the people when they sacrificed some perfect animal, generally a lamb, but it didn't have to be beaten up. The scourging Jesus suffered from the soldiers was *for our sicknesses, diseases and pains*—the divine transfer from the believer to his Savior, Substitute, Redeemer. He, the Lamb of God, bought us with his own body, which was more than any sacrifice in the Old Testament law could ever do!

So when Good Friday comes around each year, after you remember what Jesus has done for you, then thank Him, praise Him and give Him glory, and say: **"He did it for me!"** Hallelujah! To really remind yourself of what He did for you, watch *The Passion of the Christ,* or one of the other movies of the passion week of Jesus. The crucifixion scene from *The Jesus Film Project* has gotten people saved all over the world for years, even in the remotest or most dangerous locations. Many times witches, witchdoctors, and cult leaders have been saved as they watch this movie; it's that powerful!

Follow Jesus example: He got up early and went to a solitary place to pray. (Mark 1:35) He even prayed all night, and His prayers got results! When you spend this time, ask the Lord what you should do, and continue to ask Him often throughout your day. Jesus said, "For every one that asketh receiveth; and he that seeketh findeth; and to him that knocketh it shall be opened" (Luke 11:10). James 1:5–7 says we are to "ask in faith, nothing wavering." Because He said in Luke 11:17: "Every kingdom divided against itself is brought to desolation; and a house divided against a house falleth." So don't doubt after you have asked, just *believe!* Stand trusting God has heard you and will answer!

Then "Cast not away therefore your confidence, which hath great recompence of reward" (Heb. 10:35). Settle in your mind once you have spoken words of faith—it's done! Be so confident in the power of *the Word, the Name* and *the Blood* that nothing can shake you off it!

When I'm not sure and I need an answer quick, I ask: "Is it this or that?", and I go with whatever the leading is, trusting I'm hearing from Him, because Jesus said, "My sheep hear My voice and a voice of a stranger they will not follow." [That was such a blessing to me when I was not sure if I was hearing from Him.] Remind yourself of this Scripture and say: **"I hear my Father's voice and the voice a stranger I will not follow."**

This is where your time spent in the Word *and* praying in the Holy Spirit pays off. He may remind you of a Scripture or story from the Bible that fits your situation perfectly. This happens to me mostly when I'm praying in the morning, or when I'm counseling someone. What a blessing—we're never alone as the Word says.

Years ago the Holy Spirit said: *"My life would be marked with miracles."* Another thing He said in a dream was that "My mother would go to Heaven in her sleep on Friday." Years ago my mother had gotten really sick in the spring at the age of eighty-four, which sent her to the hospital. The doctor recommended she get physical therapy at a nursing home, because she kept falling backward. This was to prepare her to go back to her apartment, but she was very much against going to a nursing home!

Around this time the Holy Spirit began giving me ideas of things to do, like get a Patient Advocacy, and a Power of Attorney forms signed, etc. Next as I was passing the Post Office, I got the thought to have her mail transferred to our address; and lastly, begin making arrangements with the funeral home near us for the future.

During these few weeks, her sister and I used to stop in and see her, bring her whatever she needed and spend some time with her. Since she was getting physical therapy, she would share how well she was doing until the Thursday that I walked in, and all her things were on her bed. This was almost two weeks after my dream, which I shared with her sister and her pastor, whom she loved. I told them that they should spend whatever time they wanted with her, but the first Friday passed, and this was the next week, when she boldly said she was going home!

Following that proclamation, we were awakened the *next* morning (Friday) about 2:45 a.m., when the nursing home called and said she was gone. When we arrived there, the staff had put her Bible on her chest with her hands clasping it.

How loving of the Lord to prepare me for this difficult time in my life. If things had not been done in order, we would have had to do all the stressful things that go with the death of a family member. Everything went smoothly, because of the Holy Spirit's leading and love.

And Hezekiah rejoiced, and all the people,
that God had prepared the people:
for the thing was done suddenly.
—1 Chronicles 29:36

We need to make Scriptural faith confessions out loud on Healing, and related topics <u>every day</u>, sometimes more than once a day, if you have symptoms. When a doctor gives you a prescription, you often have to take it several times a day to deal with them. So do the same thing with the Word, which doesn't have side effects or worse. This is important, as many drugs advertised on television or in magazines have side effects, which are worse than the disease or will kill you. The Word will always do you good when you *believe*!

Speak those things that are not as thou they were just as God did (Rom. 4:17), because He says, "For I will hasten my word to perform it" (Jer.1:12b). Psalms 103:20 says, "Bless the Lord, you His angels, who excel in strength, who do His word, heeding the voice of His word." Also verse 5 referring to the Lord, "Who satisfies your mouth with good things; so that your youth is renewed like the eagles." So your confessions of the Word can bring good things, *and a renewed you*. That's a reward for your faith confessions, and another reason to do it.

We don't need to speak what we have like pain, symptoms, etc. It is pointless to state the obvious. We want to <u>enforce</u> health and wholeness, not the symptoms in our bodies. We need to <u>say what we want</u>, so what we have will change. **We get what we say!**

Speak to the mountain and command it to be cast into the sea in Jesus' Name. (Matt.17:20; Mark 11:23) Speak to those symptoms in faith (*without doubting in your heart or mind*), and cast them into the sea! Who do you think sent those symptoms—the liar, deceiver, counterfeiter himself—satan! Shake off those snake bites just like Paul did on the island of Melita. (Acts 28:5)

Luke 3:5: "Every valley shall be filled, and every mountain and hill shall be brought low; the crooked shall be made straight, and the rough ways shall be made smooth; and all flesh shall see the salvation of God." Aren't there places on your body that are crooked, rough, a mountain or a hill: like a bump, or a stubborn belly, crooked toes or backs; rough skin? Remember "All Scripture is given by inspiration of God, and is profitable . . . for correction . . . that the man of God may be perfect" (2 Tim. 3:16). So use these Scriptures in your faith confessions to improve your body.

> But he who looks into the perfect law of liberty and
> continues in it, and is not a forgetful
> hearer but a doer of the work,
> this one will be blessed in what he does.
> —James 1:25 NKJV

Disciplines of a Transformed Life:

We need to keep the atmosphere in our homes filled with Christian music and teaching, instead of news, sports, sitcoms, etc. This can be done by tuning to a Christian radio station in your area, and using Christian music tapes or CDs, especially while you spend time with the Lord, which will create a spiritual atmosphere to hear from Him. There is no distance in the Spirit when you worship Him.

> O come, let us worship and bow down;
> let us kneel before the Lord our maker.
> For he is our God;
> —Psalm 95: 6, 7a

[Terry Macalmon has two excellent worship CDs: *Live Worship*, and *I Came to Worship You*. Nothing compares to these to cause you to worship and be encouraged. I've had them for years. We put them on our IPod for when we travel, and also on my MP3 player when I walk the track at the athletic club; they automatically repeat, so you don't have to start them over and break the spirit.

I generally use them when I am reading the Word, and a different one when praying. I get more out of my reading when it is running softly in the background. It has names of God in a song, *The Lord's Prayer*, *Heal Me*, *Miracles So Great*, and more. All of them are easy to learn and sing.]

You want to create a welcoming atmosphere *to draw in the Holy Spirit* to deliver, heal, and restore your life. That is why you need 'a prayer closet', where you can spend time with the Lord <u>without interruption or distractions,</u> including from your pets. They can all wait till you're done. Let those you live with know that *this time is precious to you*, and they should only interrupt if there is an emergency or urgent need.

You don't want to lose what the Holy Spirit wants to do or tell you by an interruption, which can break the spiritual atmosphere. Remember *He is a Holy God*, and He should be respected as if you had an appointment with a king or the CEO of a huge corporation, because *He is more than that*!

However, you can talk to Him about anything on your heart, because He is your daddy, Wonderful Counselor, Mighty God, and *nothing is impossible with Him!* It's like going to the President of a major company, and he welcomes you in, clears the room and tells you to sit on His lap! How good is that!

Jesus said, "Come unto me all ye that labor and are heavy laden and I will give you rest" (Matt.11:28). Jesus is saying that whatever the problem, He has the answer that will refresh, and bring you peace.

> And it came to pass, when the minstrel played,
> that *the hand of the Lord* came upon him.
> —2 Kings 3:15b (Emphasis added)

Also, *don't rush during your time with the Lord*; allow thirty minutes to an hour in the morning, or if you don't have the time, ask God to help you get up earlier. Many times I am so awake that I have to get up, or *something* wakes me up. It could even be noise or pain that when I get up disappears. Amazing! Years ago when this first started happening, I would hear a door bell or a telephone sound, until I finally got the message: He wanted my time.

If you are not tending your 'spiritual garden', it will dry up, and then weeds will begin showing up: like getting easily angered, discouraged, gossiping, fault-finding, complaining, selfishness, etc.—all things that are not Christ-like. It's kind of like owning a beautiful lawn and garden, then the temperatures rise, there is no rain for days or weeks, then everything turns beige and dies. If you let it go too long, you will have to start all over again, which is very costly.

So keep your spirit watered by the Word daily to keep you in the plan of God for your life, "Looking unto Jesus the author and finisher of your faith" (Heb. 12:2). Just like you keep your lawn watered, fertilized and weeded, you need to *feed your spiritual life* to keep it in control and fruitful, so the bugs, spiders, and critters (anything from the enemy) doesn't sneak in, because they are not going to announce their arrival to prepare you. Be proactive and be prepared with all you need to stop him in his tracks!

If you miss your time with the Lord in the morning, you can catch up at lunch or before bed. These will be much harder to do, because the enemy will hinder you anyway he can. Just don't neglect your time with the Lord, and you will be blessed! The Bible says, "David strengthened himself in the Lord his God" (1 Sam. 30:6b NKJV) when his city was burned, their families were taken captive, and he was threatened with stoning. That's real trouble, but he knew where his only help would come from.

Before Salvation the Bible reads like Greek; after salvation, it is alive and makes sense.

You need to think about the Word, Who is Jesus, and *not just put in our time. Read it, personalize it and act on it.* Fill the recesses of your heart with the Word, the Truth, "for out of the abundance of the heart the mouth speaketh" (Matt.12:34). Your first words in a crisis could make or break it. "Proverbs 6:2: Thou art snared with the words of thy mouth, thou are taken with the words of thy mouth." Notice you are *snared* and *taken* with the words of your mouth.

So stop, *ask* for the Holy Spirit's direction, then *be obedient and prompt* regarding the instructions you get. There is an old saying that "Obedience brings blessings." As you read the Word, you will see this in various Scriptures, and people's lives.

Read the New Testament out loud, so *you see it with your eyes, hear it with your ears and get it into your heart.* Paul prays that the eyes of our (hearts) understanding be enlightened. (Eph. 1:18 NKJV) Your mind is a computer; program it with the Truth, which feeds your spirit and gives you "the mind of Christ" (1 Cor. 2:16).

The more you read the Word, you will have a greater ability to recognize His voice when He speaks to you. When He brings to your remembrance what you have read, you will have greater confidence that it is He that is guiding you. Besides, we are to *renew our minds* (Rom.12:2) with the Word from our old way of thinking. You got saved from your sins by faith, so now pick up the Way to a new life and relationship with your Lord and Savior, by reading about Him and how He thinks.

Countless times when I was praying or talking to someone, a story would come to mind from the Bible that was perfect for the situation—that's how the Holy Spirit works. He reminds you of what you have sown in your heart, and He will continue to speak to those who obey Him. (Acts 5:32) The more you hear from Him, the more you'll want to praise Him and praise Him, which brings hope, joy, and peace into your life. You can't praise Him too much. *You get blessed when you do.*

> Then they believed His words;
> they sang His praise.
> —Psalms 106:12 NKJV

Chapter 4

Only Believe: The Name!

In the story about the lame man at the gate Beautiful in Acts 3:2–8,16, Peter spoke the NAME of Jesus Christ of Nazareth, and commanded him to rise up and walk. Next, he helped him up and *immediately* his feet and ankle bones were restored, so he could both walk and leap, and praise God. Then Peter explained that it was through faith in Jesus' Name that gave him "perfect soundness". Because this man gave Peter his attention, and *expected to receive something*, he was blessed and made whole, instead of just money!

So expect to receive your "perfect soundness", by *putting all of your faith in the Person* and *Name of Jesus*, as your Lord and Savior, and especially for what He has done for you on the Cross.

"Neither is there salvation in any other: for there is none other name under heaven given among men, whereby we must be saved" (Acts 4:12). Remember salvation means deliverance, preservation, soundness, prosperity, happiness, rescue, and general well-being.

*Draw the line with the Name and Blood
of Jesus for breakthrough!*

Notice the lame man's response: he began walking, leaping and praising God. When we *believe* we have received from the Lord, we also should begin leaping and praising God, *even if it's in faith* till the manifestation comes. *Praising the Lord in faith is never wrong.* Psalms says God lives (enthroned) in the praises of His people. (Ps. 22:3)

Peter said, "If we this day be examined of the good deed done to the impotent man, by what means he has been made whole, be it known unto you all, and to all the people of Israel, that by the NAME of Jesus Christ of Nazareth, whom ye crucified, whom God raised from the dead, even by Him doth this man stand here before you whole" (Acts 4:9, 10; emphasis added). Put your name here _____, or say: "**I stand before you whole, because of the Name of Jesus!**"

From now on don't talk about how you feel, but what you *believe:* your miracle has already happened! So praise Him it has! Write it down on your calendar or journal and say: "**On this date I believed and received my miracle. So flesh line up with my confession. I don't receive the lies of the devil. Jesus is Lord and I am saved! It is as I say!**" Say it ten, twenty or fifty times if you have to. Stay focused on the Word and not your flesh!

Remember Jesus is High Priest of your confession (Heb. 3:1), so be *tenacious* and don't let go or quit! Sometimes He waits to see if we are really serious, or if we have a plan B. The disciples had to wake Him up when the storm was raging, and the boat was sinking, *before* He calmed the storm with His authority over nature *and faith,* that it would be done.

Is He hearing your persistent *belief in the Word,* or have you just let the devil have his way with you? Are you going to accept everything that comes into your life, or are you going to exercise authority and *stand for your rights as a child of God?* (Rom. 8:16) Are you going to believe the evil report of the devil, or *believe* the report of the Lord that says you were healed? Choose whom you will believe this day!

Making a Demand on the Provision

There is a story about a woman
with a large visible cancerous growth on her face,
who had made a point of contact that she was healed.
She would stand up in church each Sunday
and confess that for several weeks,
with no visible evidence. This caused
confusion in the church.
So she went home and stood in front of her mirror,
and said to the Lord "I know I'm
healed by the stripes of Jesus.
I know what the Bible says and I believe it,
so I sure would appreciate if You would
get rid of the ugly symptoms."
Suddenly the cancer fell off and hit the floor,
revealing new healthy skin!

This woman made a demand on the provision of the Word, and received her miracle.

From *365 Days of Healing* by Mark Brazee, *Harrison House* 1999; used by permission.

* * *

Peter's prayer: "Now, Lord, look on their threats, and grant to Your servants that with all boldness they may speak Your word, by stretching out Your hand to heal, and that signs and wonders may be done through the name of Your holy Servant Jesus" (Acts 4:29, 30 NKJV).

We need to learn the power in that Name and believe it! John 14:13, 14: "And whatsoever ye shall ask in my Name, that will I do, that the Father may be glorified in the Son. If ye shall ask anything in My Name, I will do it." So when I ask anything from the Lord I begin or end the request or petition with "in Jesus' Name", according to this Scripture, because I want to receive answers.

<u>Name above every name</u>: "Wherefore God also hath highly exalted Him, and given Him a name which is above every name: that at the name of Jesus every knee should bow, of things in heaven, and things on earth, and things under the earth" (Phil. 2:9).

Also Ephesians 1:21: "Far above all principality and power and might and dominion, and every name that is named, not only in this world, but also in that which is to come." The Name of Jesus reveals His character as Physician, Deliverer, Healer, Redeemer, Lord God Almighty, and is above Cancer, Arthritis, MS, Diabetes, cardiovascular diseases, every curse, or anything else that causes misery, such as poverty and lack.

John 20:30, 31: "And many other signs truly did Jesus in the presence of his disciples, which are not written in this book: but these are written, that ye might believe that Jesus is the Christ, the Son of God; and that believing ye might have life through his Name." That is why I have written so many Scriptures, so that you will *believe* to be made whole. It is with repetition that we learn and remember anything. Jesus repeatedly said, "He that believeth on me hath everlasting life" (John 6:47).

You are the master over your body, so speak to your condition and *command* symptoms to bow their knee to the Name of Jesus, and get out of your body or life! Draw the line with the **Name of Jesus!** Then command all the symptoms to flee in Jesus' Name! Pull down all the strongholds (things that are difficult to break), that are formed against health, healing and soundness manifest in your body! We are the body of Christ, His flesh and His bones (Eph. 5:30). He's not sick or in pain, neither should we be!

In the story of the withered fig tree, Jesus cursed it (when He found nothing but leaves on it), and it dried up from the roots by morning. (Mark 11:13,14, 20–22) So curse that physical disease with the same faith as Jesus did, and say, "**You _____ will not bear fruit on this body ever again in Jesus' Name!**" Then He said, "Have faith in God" (Mark 11:22). Expect God to back you up with signs, wonders and miracles. Then praise Him for deliverance of all the symptoms just *as if it happened!*

In a television commercial, you see a man riding a motorcycle with currency (in the form of bills) all over him from head to toe. Picture yourself with the Name of Jesus on you like this man from head to toe—every part, and say "**I am covered with the Name and Blood of Jesus, which makes me whole and perfect!**"

And this is His commandment:
that we should believe on the Name of His Son Jesus Christ.
—1 John 3:23a

Names:

Alpha and Omega: Revelation 22:13: "I am Alpha and Omega, the beginning and the end, the first and the last."

Almighty: Psalms 91:1 NKJV, Strong's #7706: *Shadday*: All-powerful; when it appears as 'El Shadday, it is 'God Almighty' . . . the all-sufficient God, eternally capable of being all that His people need. Footnote: There are 3 titles for God in these verses besides the personal name of the Lord: Yahweh; 'Elyon: The Most High, Shaddai: the Almighty, and 'Elohim: 'The Sublime God'.

Christ: Second Timothy 4:22 NKJV, Strong's #5547: *Christos*. The Anointed One, emphasizing the fact that the man Jesus was God's Anointed One, the promised Messiah. Matthew 16:16: "And Simon Peter answered and said, Thou art the Christ, the Son of the living God." (John 6:69 NKJV, NU: Holy One of God.)

Deliverer: The Deliverer* will come out of Zion (Rom. 11:26 NKJV). *From *Vines Complete Expository Dictionary*: rescue from danger, or release from bondage, etc.

Faithful*: "Know therefore that the Lord thy God, He is God, the *faithful God which keepeth covenant and mercy with them that love him and keep his commandments to a thousand generations" (Deut. 7:9). (*Prov. 28:20 NKJV, Strong's #530: Firmness, stability, faithfulness, fidelity, conscientiousness, steadiness, certainty; that which is permanent, enduring, steadfast.) Hebrews 10:23 NKJV: "Let us hold fast the confession of our hope without wavering, for He who promised is faithful."

God: 'Elohim: Second Kings 19:15 NKJV, Strong's #430: God in His fullness. It refers to God the Creator. Christians have long maintained that 'Elohim reveals that God has more than one part of His being. We call those distinct parts "the Father", "the Son", and "the Holy Spirit".

> First John 4: 8b, 16b: "God is love", so we
> need to look at everything with this Scripture
> in mind. God is the same in the Old Testament,
> New Testament, and now. He does not change.
> (Mal. 3:6)

For of him, and through him, and to him, are all things:
to whom be glory for ever. Amen.
—Romans 11:36

El Roi: Hebrew for "The-God-Who-Sees" (Gen.16:13 NKJV).

Healer: God says in Exodus 15:26 NKJV: "For I am the Lord who heals[7] you." Strong's #4795: Rapha: to cure, heal, repair, mend, restore health or physical healing. Rophe': one who heals, or the Hebrew word for doctor. The Bible affirms, I am Yahweh your Physician. The main idea of the verb *rapha*' is physical diseases and their divine cure.

Helper: John 15:26 NKJV, Strong's #3875: The word signifies an intercessor, comforter, helper, advocate, counselor.

I Am: "And God said unto Moses, I AM THAT I AM" (Ex. 3:14). "I am the First and I am the Last; and beside Me there

---

[7]   *Vine's Complete Expository Dictionary* says, "To heal" may be described as "restoring to normal," an act which God typically performs.

is no God" (Isa. 44:6b). "Jesus said unto them, Verily, verily, I say unto you, before Abraham was, I AM" (John 8:58). Which means He is the *ever present One*, and agrees with Hebrews 13:5c: "I will never leave thee, nor forsake thee."

Image of God: "In whom the god of this world hath blinded the minds of them which believe not, lest the light of the glorious gospel of Christ, who is the image of God, should shine on them" (2 Cor. 4: 4). Jesus said, "I and My father are one" (John 10:30).

Immanuel: Isaiah 7:14 NKJV: "Therefore the Lord Himself shall give you a sign: Behold, a virgin shall conceive, and bear a son, and shall call His name Immanuel." Literally God-with-us.

Jesus: *Vines Complete Expository Dictionary*: Jesus—was given to the Son of God in Incarnation as His personal name. 'Christ Jesus' describes the Exalted One who emptied Himself, (Phil. 2:5), and testifies to His pre-existence; 'Jesus Christ' describes the despised and rejected One Who was afterwards glorified (Phil. 2:11), and testifies to His resurrection. 'Christ Jesus' suggest His grace, 'Jesus Christ' suggests His glory.

> *Jesus*: The Greek transliteration of the Hebrew Yeshua, "He Shall Save", "Yahweh is Salvation." Phil. 4:23 NKJV

> Luke 9:35: "And there came a voice out of the cloud, saying, This is my beloved Son: hear him."

So say the Name of the Lord often, when you are in trouble, when you need help, when you need protection, when you need a friend or when you need to conquer any situation say **Jesus!**

KING of KINGS, and **LORD of LORDS**. In Revelation 19:11–16 is where you find this title for Jesus, besides Faithful and True; and The Word of God. That says it all. How can we not trust Him?

Lord: ʻ**Adonai**, a kind of plural form that is used only in reference to the glorious Lord in all His powers and attributes. Micah 4:13 NKJV, Strong's #2962: an adjective signifying authority or having *power. As a noun the word designates the owner, master, controller, one in authority. In the OT it refers to Yahweh, while in the NT the title is transferred to Jesus. (John 6:68 NKJV) (*power: 1 Tim. 6:16, Strong's #2904: Dominion, strength, manifested power especially God's kingdom authority, dominion, and majesty.) Also in 1 Corinthians 1:24c: "Christ the power of God, and the wisdom of God."

> And they that know thy Name will put their trust in thee:
> for thou, Lord, hast not forsaken them that seek thee.
> —Psalms 9:10

> But to us there is but one God, the Father,
> of whom are all things, and we in him;
> and one Lord Jesus Christ,
> by whom are all things, and we by him.
> —1 Corinthians 8:6

Lord God Almighty: "Holy, holy, holy, Lord God Almighty, Who was and is and is to come" (Rev. 4:8b). "And His name shall be called Wonderful, Counsellor, The mighty God, The everlasting Father, The Prince of Peace" (Isa. 9:6c). NKJV footnote: "The Child is God incarnate, the Omnipotent One. The word translated "Mighty" has the additional meaning of "hero." The Lord is the infinite Hero of His people, the Divine Warrior who has triumphed over sin and death."

Messiah: the **Prince**: Daniel 9:25 NKJV, Strong's #4899: *Anointed one* is Christos in Greek and is the origin of the English form "Christ." Whenever the Lord is called "Jesus Christ," He is being called "Messiah the Prince".

Physician: "And he said unto them, Ye will surely say unto me this proverb, Physician, heal thyself'" (Luke 4:23a).

Prince of Peace: Isaiah 9:6 NKJV footnote: His reign will be characterized by *shalom*: health, well-being, prosperity, happiness, and cessation of enmity. "For He Himself is our peace" (Eph. 2:14 NKJV). That is everything we need. So when someone says to you "Shalom", they are blessing you.

> In the book of Judges 6:24 NKJV footnote, Gideon built an altar to the Lord and called it The-Lord-Is-Peace, which literally means Yahweh Shalom[8]: wholeness, security, prosperity, peace, and friendship.

Redeemer: Christ hath redeemed[9] us from "the curse" of the law (Deut. 28:15–68), being made a curse for us: for it is written, Cursed is every one that hangeth on a tree (Gal. 3:13, 14). This is what was done for us on the cross, because of Jesus obedience to take the brutal, scourging, *punishment on His own body for us*, so we could be made whole.

---

[8] Complete; having nothing missing.
[9] Neh. 1:4, Strong's #6299: To release, preserve, rescue, deliver, liberate, cut loose, sever; to free; to ransom.

Isaiah 54:5: "For thy Maker is thine husband; the Lord of hosts is His name; and thy Redeemer the Holy One of Israel; the God of the Whole earth shall he be called." Nehemiah 1:10: "Now these are thy servants and thy people, whom thou hast redeemed by thy great power, and by thy strong hand."

In Deuteronomy 26:8, God brought Israel "out of Egypt with a mighty hand and with an out-stretched arm, with great terribleness[10], and with signs and with wonders" [such as frogs, and plagues, darkness and death that only He could control.] But in the New Testament, He sent Jesus to die on the cross *with outstretched arms for us*, and many signs and wonders followed that will never be forgotten! "He Himself took our infirmities and bore our sicknesses" (Matt. 8:17 NKJV, which refers to Isa. 53:5).

Restorer: In Matthew 12:13, Mark 8:25, Jesus healed the man with the withered hand and made it whole; and also the blind man at Bethsaida, which the Word says He will do in Jeremiah 30:17 NKJV, "For I will restore health to you and heal you of your wounds, says the Lord." Joel 2:25 NKJV footnote: as part of an era when both physical and spiritual needs will be met: "I will restore to you the years that the locust hath eaten." This tells us that restoration is coming.

---

[10]   To their enemy

In Isaiah 42:22 NKJV, the Word says: "But this is a people robbed and plundered; all of them are snared in holes, and they are hidden in prison (houses of bondage); they are for prey, and no one delivers; for plunder, and no one says, "Restore!" So if you are not saying *restore*, you don't get it. Since Jesus is our Restorer, ask Him to restore all you have been robbed of: health, peace, joy, finances, friends, etc.

God *restored* Moses hand in Exodus 4:6, 7: "And the Lord said furthermore unto him, Put now thine hand into thy bosom. And he put his hand into his bosom: and when he took it out, behold, his hand was leprous as snow. And he said, Put thine hand into thy bosom again. And he put his hand into his bosom again; and plucked it out of his bosom, and, behold, it was turned again as his other flesh." This was one of the "signs" Moses was supposed to show Pharaoh that God had sent him. Notice how quickly his hand was *restored* when he obeyed the Lord.

Savior: "For if, after they have escaped the pollutions of the world through the knowledge of the Lord and Savior Jesus Christ." Second Peter 2:20a NKJV, *Savior*–Strong's #4990: The Word designates a deliverer, preserver, *savior*, benefactor, rescuer. It is used to describe both **God** the Father and **Jesus** the Son.

Shepherd: "I am the good shepherd" (John 10:11). John 10:2 NKJV, Strong's #4166: one who tends, leads, guides, cherishes, feeds and protects a flock. Psalms 23:1AB: "The Lord is my shepherd [to feed, guide, and shield me], I shall not lack." So if we lack health in any part of our body, He is our Shepherd. Jesus is talking about the benefits of his being our Good Shepherd, which includes protection, abundant life and provision. He is our security and safety when we listen to Him. Continually confess: **"The Lord is my Shepherd and I shall not want**." in the face of every need.

Sun of Righteousness: "But to you who fear my name The Sun of Righteousness shall arise with healing in his wings." Malachi 4:2 NKJV, Strong's #4832: Restoration of health, remedy, cure, medicine; tranquility, deliverance, refreshing.

The Lord Who Breaks Out, or Breaks Through: In Second Samuel 5:17-25 NKJV, David inquired of the Lord whether he should go out against the Philistines, the enemy. God said He'd deliver them into his hand, which He did. Then David said, "The Lord has broken through my enemies before me, like a breaking out of great waters. So he called the name of that place Baal Perazim." Footnote: The Lord (in this case Yahweh) Who Breaks Out," or "The Lord Breaks Through."[11]

> When you have been struggling with something for a long time, do you think God would do any less for you as His child? So inquire of the Lord for His perfect will for you, take His counsel and go forward *believing* He will back you up. Then give Him glory for what He has done.

---

[11] Jerry Savelle of *Jerry Savelle Ministries* has a book called *'The God of the Breakthrough Will Visit Your House'*.

The Way, the Truth, and the Life: "Jesus said to him, I am the Way, the Truth and the Life; no one comes to the Father except by (through) Me" (John 14:6 AB). NKJV footnote: Jesus is **the way . . . to the Father**. He is **the truth** about God and the very **life** of God. As such, He reveals truth to us and gives life to us. [This is a great Scripture to be shared with a person of another religion, as the Lord leads.]

Who is able: Jude 24NKJV, Strong's #1410: The word combines power and willingness, inherent strength and action. Second Chronicles 25:9b, "The Lord is able to give thee much more than this." Daniel 3:17: "If it be so, our God whom we serve is able to deliver us from the burning fiery furnace." Matthew 9:28c: "And Jesus saith unto them, Believe ye that I am able to do this?" Second Corinthians 9:8: "And God is able to make all grace abound toward you." Second Timothy 1:12: "For I know whom I have believed, and am persuaded that he is able to keep that which I have committed unto him against that day."

The Word: "In the beginning was the Word, and the Word was with God, and the Word was God. And the Word was made flesh and dwelt among us, (and we beheld his glory, the glory as of the only begotten of the Father,) full of grace and truth" (John 1:1,14). "For there are three that bear record in heaven, the Father, the Word, and the Holy Ghost: and these are one" (1 John 5:7). "And his name is called The Word of God" (Rev.19:13).

Yah: "For Yah, the Lord, is my strength and song; He also has become my salvation" (Isa.12:2). NKJV, Strong's #3050: The shorter form of the Lord's Holy name Yahweh, or Jehovah. Hallelu-Yah, translated "Praise the Lord".

But these are written, that ye might believe that
Jesus is the Christ, the son of God;
and that believing ye might have life through his name.
—John 20:31

Chapter 5

Only Believe:
He is Worthy to be Worshipped!

Psalms 100:4, 5 NKJV:

> "Enter into His gates with thanksgiving, and
> into His courts with [praise]; be thankful unto
> Him, and bless His name. For the Lord is good;
> His mercy is everlasting, and His truth endureth
> to all generations."

Praise: NKJV Strong's #8416 means a celebration, a lauding of someone praise-worthy; the praise or exaltation of God; praises, songs of admiration. See Psalms 136:1–9 also. 1 Chronicles 23:30 NKJV, Strong's #1984: usually conveys the idea of speaking or singing about the glories, virtues, or honor of someone or something. When King David was giving the orders for the Levites, he said, "To stand every morning to thank and praise the Lord, and likewise at even;" Should we do any less when Jesus has provided so much for us?

Revelation 5:11b, 12, 13:

> And the number of them was ten thousand
> times ten thousand and thousands of thousands
> [of angels] saying with a loud voice, Worthy is

the Lamb that was slain to receive power, and riches, and wisdom, and strength, and honour, and glory and blessing. And every creature which is in heaven . . . Blessing and honour and glory, and power, be unto Him that sitteth up on the throne, and unto the Lamb forever and ever.

Should we do any less who are the ones He was slain for?

Our Good Deliverer: "Oh, give thanks to the Lord, for He is good: for His mercy endureth for ever." Psalms 107:1, 6, 8, 9: "Then they cried unto the Lord in their trouble, and He delivered them out of their distresses." (Repeated four times) "Oh, that men would praise the Lord for His goodness, and for His wonderful works to the children of men! For He satisfieth the longing soul, and fills the hungry soul with goodness." Verse 20: "He sent His word and healed them, and delivered them from their destructions." Verse 38: "He blesseth them also, so that they multiplied greatly." Verse 43: "Whoso is wise, will observe these things, even they shall understand the lovingkindness of the Lord."

"O Lord, great and awesome God, who keeps His covenant and mercy with those who love Him, and with those who keep His commandments" (Dan. 9:4b NKJV).

"For He Himself has said, "I will never leave you nor forsake you. So we may boldly say: 'The Lord is my **helper**'" (Heb.13: 5b, 6a NKJV). No fear here!

"O Lord our Lord*, how excellent is Your name in all the earth! who hast set thy glory above the heavens. Out of the mouth of babes and sucklings hast thou ordained strength (better translated *praise*, NKJV) because of thine enemies, that thou mighest still the enemy and the avenger" (Ps. 8:1, 2 NKJV *Master Sovereign). Notice it says that *praise stills the enemy and the avenger.* Wouldn't "still" mean he would be quiet; so he can't lie or deceive us? That's a good thing. Then why would he stay around? Probably not!

Hebrews 2:14, 15 (Amplified):

> Since, therefore, [these His] children share in flesh and blood [in the physical nature of human beings], He [Himself] in a similar manner partook of the same [nature], that by [going through] death He might bring to nought *and* make of no effect him who had the power of death—that is, the devil—and also that He might deliver *and* completely set free all those who through the [haunting] fear of death were held in bondage throughout the whole course of their lives.

He is worthy to be worshipped, because as a human being He went through death on the cross to bring to nothing (nought) the devil, who had the power of death, so that we would be delivered and completely set free from the haunting fear of death, which had held us in bondage our whole lives.

"Fear of death" is a master fear and affects other ways we react to things like: fear of people; fear of heights, fear of animals, fear of stepping out to do something, etc. You can get rid of it by *casting it out in the Name of Jesus,* and purposely replacing it with the promises of God, already discussed. Unfortunately the enemy is persistent, so you may have to do this as needed and to clear your mind.

Because of Jesus obedience to take *sins by faith* on Himself to the cross, He made it possible for no one to have to go to hell if they *believed.* Psalms 22:1: "My God, my God, why hast thou forsaken me?" Hell is total separation from God as a punishment for unrepented sin, a state of being forsaken. Jesus went through this hell experience in our place for our sins, so we will not have to.

Because of Jesus *bringing to nought the devils' power,* he can only threaten people—nothing else to a Believer. It is written in 1 John 4:18, "There is no fear in love; but perfect love casteth out fear; because fear hath torment. He that feareth is not made perfect in love." Verse 16: "And we have known and believed the love that God hath to us. God is love; and he that dwelleth in love dwelleth in God, and God in him."

Practice *seeing yourself in Jesus—God, and then Jesus in you*—what could be better protection? Nothing! Then remind the enemy that **God loves YOU**, resist the devil and he has to flee, which stops the fear. Even if you have to *say it over and over again,* until *you* believe it! *Speak those things that are not until YOU are convinced,* which will cause you to praise and praise and praise Him.

Death is swallowed up in victory.
But thanks be to God,
which giveth us the victory through our Lord Jesus Christ.
—1 Corinthians 15:54d, 57

He is especially worthy to be worshipped, because of how brutally He was beaten and scourged before He went to the cross *with our* sicknesses and diseases: *infirmities* (the thirty-nine stripes) that he said his bones were out of joint, and he could count them. (Matt. 8:17; Ps. 22:14, 17) He knew these Psalms verses and others (Isa. 52:14; 53:2) were prophesied years before, yet He suffered any way for us!

Believe He paid the price. Focus on His perfect finished work on the cross, because *He loves you*, so you can say: **"Disease has no right in my body. By Jesus stripes I have been healed of every form of sickness, disease or curse! I claim my rights to the finished work of the cross today. He did it for me!"**

How can you not praise and worship Him every day for what He has done for you? "Because thy lovingkindness is better than life, my lips shall praise thee. Thus will I bless thee while I live: I will lift up my hands in thy name. Let us lift up our heart with our hands unto God in the heavens" (Ps. 63:3, 4; Lam. 3:41). Even if you are the only one in your church, remember what He has done for *you*, and worship Him with up-lifted hands when there are songs of praise and worship to Him. It's Scriptural! <u>He deserves the honor and glory!</u>

> God is greatly to be feared in
> the assembly of the saints,
> and to be held in reverence of all
> *those* that are about him.
> —Psalms 89:7 NKJV

"My soul shall be satisfied as with marrow and fatness; and my mouth shall praise thee with joyful lips" (Ps. 63:5). David wrote this when he was in the wilderness of Judah, *before* he got to the finished palace built for him. Notice he said his lips, his *up-lifted hands*, his *mouth* and again his *joyful lips*. This is an example of the "sacrifice of praise".

In the story of the woman, who came to Jesus at the Pharisee's house in Luke 7; 37, 38; 44–46, Jesus says about her actions: "Seest thou this woman? I entered into thine house, thou gavest me no water for my feet: but she hath washed my feet with tears, and wiped them with the hairs of her head. Thou gavest me no kiss: but this woman since the time I came in hath not ceased to kiss my feet. My head with oil thou didst not anoint: but this woman hath anointed my feet with ointment."

This was a dramatic scene of this woman's humility, faith, love, and honor for Jesus. She gave her all: her tears, her hair, and her ointment to bless him. As a reward, she received forgiveness of her sins and peace from him.

Have you ever shown Jesus your appreciation for: *your* forgiveness of sins, and his dying a horrible death for you on the cross, when you worship him?

Does He know *your* gratitude?

Do you thank Him for his obedience to suffer for you, to redeem you from all the curses?

Do you worship Him for all the times He saved you from some accident or disaster the enemy planned for your life?

Do you thank Him for getting you to your current age, when so many lives have been cut off at a much younger age, because *He loves you*?

Do you just worship Him just because He loves you?

Do you thank Him for taking care of you and your loved ones with a home, and meeting your needs?

Do you thank Him for the times you were blessed with a surprise? (That was His love working.)

Even though *It's a Wonderful Life* is not my favorite movie, we need to watch it each year to remind ourselves what life would be like without the Lord's care.

In Second Chronicles 20:1–30, three elements put God's people in the place where He could deliver them: fasting (v. 3), prayer (vv. 4–13) and *praise* (vv. *21, 22 *"Praise the Lord, for His mercy endures forever.") Not only were *their enemies defeated*, but they also came away with spoil, which took three days to gather, because there was so much. So there are rewards for praising God: your enemies defeated and blessings!

Psalms 29:1, 2 NKJV: "Give unto the Lord, O you mighty ones, give unto the Lord *glory and strength. Give unto the Lord the *glory due His name; *worship the Lord in the beauty of holiness." So testify regularly to God's goodness in your life. (*Worship*, Psalms 99:5, Strong's #7812–To bow, to stoop; to bow down before someone as an act of submission or reverence; to fall or bow down when paying homage to God . . . bow yourselves down low before Him at the place of His feet.)

*Glory, *doxa:*[12] In John 2:11 NKJV: it becomes splendor, radiance, and majesty centered in Jesus. [Close your eyes and just picture Him like this description.] Here *doxa* is the majestic, absolute perfection residing in Christ and evidenced by the miracles He performed.

Praise Him continually

---

[12] Strong's #3519 – Weightiness; that which is substantial or heavy; honor, splendor, power, wealth, authority, magnificence, fame, dignity, riches, and excellency. (Is. 60:1 NKJV) Worshipful praise, thanksgiving; giving glory to God. *Merriam-Webster Inc*

Hebrews 13:15: "By him therefore let us offer the sacrifice of praise to God continually, that is, the fruit of our lips, giving thanks to His name." Note: *Practice persistent and patient praise.* Learn simple choruses of praise to the Lord, or make them up. Tell Him who He is to you: your Savior, Healer, Deliverer, Redeemer, Counselor, High Priest of your Confession, . . .

Jesus said: "But the hour cometh, and now is, when the true worshippers shall worship the Father in spirit and in truth: for the Father seeketh such to worship him. God is a spirit: and they that worship him must worship him in spirit and truth" (John 4:23). Since Jesus made this statement to bless you and God, why wouldn't you do it? Obedience brings blessings—the Presence of God!

Now it sounds quite clear to me, but to explain: since God is a Spirit, in order to make perfect contact with Him as He wants, we must worship spirit to spirit. The only way you can do that is with spiritual language or songs, the prayer language you received when you asked to be baptized in the Spirit. That is the first thing the disciples did at Pentecost: "We hear them speak in our tongues the wonderful works of God" (Acts 2:11).

Also, worshipping in truth is sincere, from the heart, speaking your own words of praise to God your father. So say often 'Hallelujah, hallelujah!' as you are praising. Learn the names of the Lord and what they mean, so you can use them while worshiping Him, *and* for the specific area you need help with in your life, like Jehovah Jireh (Provider), Jehovah Rapha (Healer); our Redeemer, our Intercessor, our Counselor, Mighty God, and Prince of Peace. *He is our All-in-All!*

Is He to you? If not, begin seeking Him with all your heart and soul and strength and mind, and He will be found. Read Job 38–41 to see something of His Omnipotence. Go to your concordance and look up every Scripture that describes **God**; it is worth your time!

Read the four gospels to see Him in the Person of Jesus Christ—the Word made flesh. "Who is the image of the invisible God, the firstborn of every creature: For by Him were all things created, that are in heaven, and that are on earth, visible and invisible, whether they be thrones, or dominions or principalities or powers: all things were created by Him and for Him. And He is before all things, and by Him all things consist" (Col. 1:15-17).

Notice His wisdom, His ability to handle any situation that was brought to Him, how often He taught and then delivered the oppressed of the devil, or healed them. If He did it for them, then He can do it for us also.

> He came that we may have life and they
> may have it more abundantly.
> —John 10:10b NKJV

> He is the "yes" and Amen to all the promises of God.
> —2 Corinthians 1:20

> He is the Apostle and High Priest of our confession.
> —Hebrews 3:1 NKJV

> Jesus Christ the same yesterday, to day, and for ever.
> —Hebrews13:8

He is precious to those who believe.
—1 Peter 2:7

He takes our cares, because He cares for us.
—1 Peter 5:7

He was manifested that he might
destroy the works of the devil.
—1 John 3:8b

We need to spend time everyday worshipping and praising the Lord for who He is, and thanking Him for what He has done in our life. If you are reading this, you are blessed: you had the money to buy the book, a vehicle to get to a store, or a computer to order it from, etc.

Praise establishes a line of communication with our Lord. *Get involved in worship.* Think of Him standing *in front of you. Visualize Him* from how He is described in the Word. This will change your whole attitude about how you worship. Picture Him as the Good Shepherd carrying His sheep. We are His sheep. He is Captain of the Host of the Lord. When Joshua met Him, he fell on his face to the earth and *worshiped!* (Josh. 5:13–15)

In Ezra 8:2, Jesus is seen as a fire from the loins up and from the loins down. He is holy and the Creator of all things. **He is All Mighty God!** What would you do if you could see Him directly in front of you? The twenty-four elders in Revelation 4:10, eleven fell down before His throne and threw their crowns at His feet crying "Thou art worthy, O Lord to receive glory and honor and power." Amen!

Power of Praise

Faithful Father Finally Blessed

In his sermon, <u>It's Time to Receive Your Restoration</u>*,
Pastor Prince, shares about a man whose
daughter had been in an accident
and was brain-damaged, even to the point of slobbering.
This father visited her each month for <u>seven years</u>
in the intensive care area in a mental
institution (behind a steal door)
even though she did not recognize or
respond to him or others.
She had been prayed for by the Full
Gospel Business Men's group and
well meaning others, but there was no change.
Then in the seventh year, as he drove to visit her,
he began to complain to the Lord saying things like:
"How can You do this Lord—being a God of love?"

This is where Pr. Prince adds, "Now
we all know it's not God . . .
when things go wrong we always want to blame God . . .
but God is not interested in who's wrong: He's
interested in *restoring your future.*"

Then this father, who became angry at God said,
"I can't understand this"; but he heard "Praise Me".

Then he argued "No way when my
daughter is in a mental institution,
because she is so bad". But he heard again: "Praise Me."
So even though it didn't make sense, his heart melted,
he surrendered to the Lord, and began
praising Him on his way to her room,
when suddenly he heard a scream "I want
My daddy, I want my daddy!"
Then she burst through the door to embrace him,
and she was restored in an instant!

Pr. Prince shared this extreme story to show that <u>all the prayers did not achieve what those few minutes of praise did.</u> He also said that he had heard on the News that the longest living people of any profession are in the music industry, because choir directors spend their time *raising their hands to conduct,* similar to when the referee confirms a touchdown, we shoot up our hands to declare the victory!

*Sept. 27, 2009, Used by permission. For more information, visit Joseph Prince.com

* * *

So why wait? *Declare the victory over your symptoms now by faith!*

Praise Delivers from TB

From "Seven Things You Should Know
About Divine Healing",
a young man was healed of TB in the last stages!
The story begins with a young, married, traveling
Evangelist, who discovered he had TB.
So everywhere he went he asked people to pray for him,
including the leading healing Evangelists of
his day but he continued to get worse,
until he became bedfast (hemorrhaging
from both lungs) wasting away.
One day while he was looking out the
window at his father-in-law's farm,
he decided to get himself over to the
clump of trees and bushes,
about a quarter of a mile away, and
pray until he was healed or die.
Next he asked the Lord for help and he started off.
He reached the destination and then laid down to rest.
That's when he thought of all the thousands
of people that had prayed for him,
and that if prayer was going to do it, he
should have been healed by now.
So he thought he needed something else besides prayer,
and remembered he had never believed he received
when he had been prayed for (Mark 11:24).
Then he realized he had missed it.

*He'd been trying to get God to give
him what was already his.
He was so weak he couldn't talk above a whisper,
and the devil harassed him about that.
So he began in a whisper praising the
Lord that he received his healing,
which caused him to get strong enough to prop himself up.
Next he put his hands in the air, as he
continued to praise in faith,
because he believed he received his
healing when he was prayed for.
At the end of an hour and a half, he
was standing on his feet,
hollering "Praise God" so loudly, people
heard him two miles away,
and he was healed!*

Kenneth Hagin, *Kenneth Hagin Ministries,*
used by permission

* * *

Ezra 3:12, 13: Regarding the laying of the foundation of the temple, "Many shouted aloud for joy, so that the people could not discern the noise of the shout of joy from the noise of the weeping of the people, for the people shouted with a loud shout, and the noise was heard afar off." The difference was that this Evangelist did something he hadn't done yet: _Believed_ he *received his healing by faith,* and praise God for it, till it was manifested!

As you can see from these two testimonies, when there was no other way, praising the Lord in faith without ceasing, changed the situation and brought the healing.

Chapter 6

Only Believe:
It's God's Will to Heal You!

"Oh how great is Thy goodness, which Thou hast laid up for them that fear Thee; which Thou hast wrought for them that trust in Thee before the sons of men!" (Ps. 31:19)

"The goodness of God endureth continually" (Ps. 52:1b).

"Surely goodness and mercy shall follow me all the days of my life" (Ps. 23:6).

"And He said, I will make all my goodness pass before thee, and I will proclaim the name of the Lord before thee; and will be gracious to whom I will be gracious, and will shew mercy on whom I will shew mercy" (Ex. 33:19).

"And the Lord passed by before him, and proclaimed, The Lord, The Lord God, merciful and gracious, longsuffering, and abundant in goodness and truth" (Ex. 34:6).

Goodness means in the sense of what is upright, righteous; in the sense of kindness of heart or act, said of God.[13] So because of God's *goodness*, He desires for us to be healthy all our lives, and has provided the means to establish His desire for us to be healed, and even calls Himself Jehovah Rapha: "If you diligently heed the voice of the Lord your God and do what

---

[13] *Vine's Complete Expository Dictionary*

is right in His sight, give ear to His commandments and keep all this statutes, I will put none of the diseases on you which I have brought on the Egyptians, for I am the Lord who heals you" (Ex.15:26).[14]

"And the Lord will take away from thee all sickness and will put none of the evil diseases of Egypt [world], which thou knowest, upon thee; but will lay them upon all them that hate thee" (Deut. 7:15).

"And ye shall serve the Lord your God, and He shall bless thy bread and thy water; and I will take sickness away from the midst of thee . . . the number of thy days I will fulfill" (Ex.23:25, 26b).

"No good thing will He withhold from them that walk uprightly" (Ps. 84:11c). "But they that seek the Lord shall not want any good thing" (Ps. 34:10b). Healing is a "good thing" to someone who needs it. It's the most important thing!

"Bless (affectionately, gratefully praise) the Lord, O my soul, and forget not [one of] all His benefits—Who forgives [every one of] all your iniquities, Who heals [each one of] all your diseases, Who redeems your life from the pit *and* corruption, Who beautifies, dignifies, *and* crowns you with loving-kindness and tender mercy; Who satisfies your mouth [your necessity and desire at your personal age and situation] with good so that your youth, renewed, is like the eagle's [strong, overcoming, soaring]!" (Ps. 103: 2–5 AB)

---

[14]   NKJV, Strong's #7495: *heals: rapha'* means to cure, heal, repair, mend, restore health. The main idea is physical healing. Scripture affirms, "I am Yahweh your Physician."

This could mean two things: the food you eat renews your youth, or the confessions of your mouth of health, restoration, etc. renews your youth. I prefer to use the later.

So this says "benefits" include *forgiveness of iniquities/sins, healing all our diseases,* redemption from a life of destruction or ruin; besides the "benefits" *of His loving-kindness,* tender mercies, *good things,* and *renewal of our youth!* So here is another reason to praise Him every day for the blessings of favor, surprises, things going well, being in the right place at the right time, and so much more. That sounds like what a loving father would do—bless us!

"Then they cry unto the Lord in their trouble, and He saveth them out of their distresses. He sent His Word and healed them, and delivered them from their destructions" (Ps. 107: 19, 20), which could be poor choices, thoughts, actions and disobedience.

As you can see by all these Scriptures, that God wanted us healed so much that He sent the Word, Jesus, to deliver us from all the infirmities that destroy our bodies, by taking them on His body on the cross. God didn't just respond with another promise, but sent the perfect answer—Jesus! "By whose stripes ye [were] healed." So it's not a future event, but a past event that we praise Him for, as if He had given us a gift from His heart. Now take it, for it was purchased at a high price, and thank Him continually.

"That He might present it to himself a glorious church, not having spot, or wrinkle, or any such thing; but that it should be holy and without blemish" (Eph. 5:27). If God wants a church without blemish and we are part of the church, then we should agree with God to be without physical spots, wrinkles, or blemishes. [I've added this to my faith confessions.] "For we are members of His body, of His flesh, and of His bones" (Eph. 5:30). We are free of all sickness and pain, because Jesus took (Matt. 8:17) it from us and carried it away to hell. He paid the price! And also, "As He is, so are we in this world" (1 John 4:17). As He is healthy and whole in Heaven, so are we—Believers—on earth.

The Lord's Prayer

Jesus said in Matthew 6:7–13:

> But when ye pray, use not vain repetitions, as the heathen do: for they think that they shall be heard for much speaking. Be not ye therefore like unto them: for your Father knoweth what things ye have need of, before ye ask Him. After this manner, therefore, pray ye: Our Father which art in heaven, hallowed be thy name. Thy kingdom come. Thy will be done in earth, as it is in heaven. Give us this day our daily bread. And forgive us our debts, as we forgive our debtors. And do not lead us into temptation, but deliver us from evil: For thine is the kingdom, and the power and the glory, for ever. Amen

We should go to God, our Heavenly father, Who is "love", reverencing Him for Who He is and praising Him for it. That's why we need to know about Him and what He can do, has done and what He has promised to do through His Word. Because I have learned and taught on the names of God, Jesus and the

Holy Spirit, I have words to worship and praise for Him with, when I begin my day in my prayer closet/office.

I pray fervently that God's kingdom come, God's will be done on earth as it is in Heaven, where there is no enemy, killing, stealing, strife, jealousy, greed, pride, fear, disease or lack of any kind; only harmony, peace, love, kindness, health, joy—bliss. **God's will be done on earth as it is in Heaven! Amen: so be it!**

Notice Jesus comments in verses 14 and 15 about forgiving others—*debtors.*[15] [Many people have not received their healing, because they have not forgiven someone, sometimes for years, who has offended them in some way.]

"For if ye forgive men their trespasses, your heavenly Father will also forgive you. But if ye do forgive not men their trespasses, neither will your father forgive your trespasses" (Matt. 6:14, 15). Don't let any unforgiveness in your life continue—<u>forgive</u>! If God leads you, go to that person, and talk to them. If not, *forgive them by faith.* Sometimes people don't know there is a problem, and speaking to them could stir up a worse problem. So ask God what to do.

> Follow peace with all men, and holiness,
> without which no man shall see the Lord.
> —Hebrews 12:14

Harboring unforgiveness only hurts you, which you can see from the Scripture above. Unforgiveness is not worth it! Many times the other person doesn't know or care anything about the

---

[15] From Luke 13:4 NKJV, Strong's #3781: A *debtor,* one who owes a moral obligation, an offender, a delinquent, a moral transgressor.

situation. Joyce Meyer says "Unforgiveness is like drinking poison and expecting the other person to die." [That person needs their head examined.]

Make it a habit to <u>forgive immediately</u>! Don't store up in your memory bank the things careless, selfish, greedy people have done to you, and *stop talking about it*, or rehashing it, so it will fade away. Purposely forget the details; even plead *the Blood of Jesus* over your conscious, sub-conscious, unconscious mind and emotions by faith. Don't allow your mind to go there again. *Change the subject; think on Jesus.*

Also, do this with a loss of any kind; forget those things that are behind. Don't mourn the loss for a long time; it will only lead to Depression. Grief is not of God. So don't allow any foothold of the devil to keep you in some bondage, or attack you in the future with some kind of misery. (See *Exercise Your Power & Authority* regarding PTSD)

> For God has not given us a spirit of fear,
> but of power and of love and
> of calm and well-balanced mind and
> discipline and self-control.
> —2 Timothy 1:7 AB

If you still think you can't forgive, see those circumstances in your hands, dig a hole in the ground *in your imagination*, and bury them! Then plant Forget-me-nots on top of the spot, and *never talk* about them again. If you do, you haven't forgiven, so just say "**On _____ I dealt with that and it's done— finished!**" Then praise God it's in His Hands.

Hebrews 13:15 NKJV: "By Him therefore let us offer the *sacrifice[16] of praise to God continually, that is, the fruit of our lips, giving thanks to His name." I repeat *practice persistent and patient praise!* This means doing it when you don't feel like it.

The Lord *restored twice* as much as Job had before, when he prayed for his friends, not when he complained, reasoned or agreed with them. He forgave them by praying for them. (Job 42:10)[17]

> Thou shalt love thy neighbor as thyself.
> —Romans 13: 9

God's Will –

"How God anointed Jesus of Nazareth with the Holy Ghost and with power, Who went about doing good and healing all that were oppressed by the devil, for God was with Him" (Acts 10:38).

"He that spared not His own Son, but delivered Him up for us all, how shall He not with Him also freely give us all things?" (Rom. 8:32) *All* could mean physically, spiritually, financially, materially, and relationally—a better life.

"The Spirit of the Lord is upon Me, because He has anointed Me to preach the gospel to the poor; He has sent Me to heal the

---

16 Praise often requires that we "kill" our pride, fear, or sloth—anything that threatens to diminish or interfere with our worship of the Lord.

17 18 NKJV, Strong's 6419: *Prayed* here means entreat, intercede, make supplication. Asking someone with more power and wisdom to intervene in behalf of the one praying.

brokenhearted, to proclaim liberty to the captives and recovery of sight to the blind, to set at liberty those who are oppressed [downtrodden]; to proclaim the acceptable year of the lord" (Luke 4:18, 19 NKJV).

In the story of the paralytic who was brought by his *friends of faith* to Jesus through the roof, Jesus said: "Son, I forgive your sins." [This upset the religious folk.] Then He said: "Why are you so skeptical? Which is simpler to say to the paraplegic, 'I forgive your sins', or say 'Get up and take your stretcher, and start walking?' Well just so it is clear that I am the Son of Man and are authorized to do either, or both . . . " (Mark 2:5, 9–11 MSG)

He was saying that *forgiveness and healing are a package deal through Him: just as saved as healed!* So the paralytic got up and left—amazing them all. Hallelujah![18] This man received it all just as each person that has received Jesus as their Savior does. So our confession should be **"I'm just as healed as I am saved!"**

Just as surely as: "For whosoever shall call upon the name of the Lord shall be saved." is in Romans 10:13; "By whose stripes ye were healed." is in 1 Peter 2:24. They are both written to be *believed* and acted upon.

---

[18]   *Salvation:* Acts 28:28 NKJV, Strong's #4992: is an all-inclusive word signifying forgiveness, healing, prosperity, deliverance, safety, rescue, liberation, and restoration

Chapter 7

Only Believe:
Jesus Did the Will of God

For I came down from heaven, not to do mine own will, but the will of Him that sent me. And this is the Father's will which hath sent me, that of all which He hath given me I should lose nothing, but should raise it up again at the last day. And this is the will of Him that sent me, that every one which seeth the Son, and believeth on him, may have everlasting life: and I will raise him up at the last day.
—John 6:38, 39

Jesus over and over again taught Scriptures, so that people would *Believe* and act on their faith to receive their miracle. That is why there are so many Scriptures in *Only Believe!*

"And Jesus went about all Galilee, teaching in their synagogues, preaching the gospel of the kingdom, and healing all kinds of sickness and all kinds of disease among the people. Then His fame went throughout all Syria; and they brought to Him all sick people who were afflicted with various diseases and torments, and those who were demon-possessed, epileptics, and paralytics; and He healed them" (Matt. 4:23, 24 NKJV). Nothing was impossible!

Even while Jesus was teaching, *the power of the Lord*, which is equivalent to the Spirit of the Lord (Who is the Holy Spirit), was present to heal them. He is the powerhouse that gets things done. The Holy Spirit is the One that causes the manifestation of the healing we need and everything else.

"And behold, a leper came and worshiped Him, saying, Lord, if You are willing, You can make me clean. Then Jesus put out His hand and touched him, saying, I am willing; be cleansed. Immediately his leprosy was cleansed" (Matt. 8:2, 3 NKJV). Notice the leper came to Jesus (which he was forbidden to do), probably because he had heard of the miracles He did. First he worshiped Him *saying words of faith*, next *Jesus touched him* saying He was willing to heal him; then *Jesus made a faith command*: **be cleansed**! And the leper was immediately healed! The leper was rewarded for his faith and respect for who Jesus is.

Jesus Heals a Centurion's Servant: "Then Jesus said to the centurion, 'Go your way; and as you have believed, so let it be done for you.' And his servant was healed that same hour" (Matt. 8:13 NKJV). Notice the servant was healed that same hour! Jesus spoke of this man as having "great faith". (v.10)

"And when Jesus was come into Peter's house, He saw his wife's mother laid, sick of a fever. And He touched her hand, and the fever left her: and she arose and ministered unto them"* (Matt. 8:14, 15). [*Proof she was healed.] Luke 4:39 says, "And He stood over her, and rebuked the fever; and it left her . . ." He commanded a symptom (the fever) and it left. So painful symptoms are from evil spirits and can be rebuked.[19] (This

---

[19]   to criticize sharply, . . . to reprimand. *Merriam-Webster Inc*

story is related to Matt. 8:26b: "Then He arose and [20]rebuked the winds and the sea; and there was a great calm.")

"When evening had come, they brought to Him many who were demon-possessed. And He cast out the spirits with a word, and healed all who were sick, [that it might be fulfilled] which was spoken by Isaiah the prophet saying: He Himself took our infirmities and bore our sicknesses" (Matt. 8:16, 17 NKJV). In all the cases just prior to this verse, it was <u>physical healings</u> that Jesus dealt with by speaking to or touching people that He went to, heard about, or were brought to him. **Jesus can do anything**! No case is too hard for Him— even yours!

That same Jesus that had *compassion* on the widow and raised her son up from the dead, also healed Jairus's daughter: "And, behold, there cometh one of the rulers of the synagogue, Jairus by name; and when he saw Him he fell at this feet, and besought Him greatly, saying, My little daughter lieth at the point of death: I pray thee, come and lay thy hands on her, that she may be healed; and she shall live." Verse 35: "While he yet spake, there came from the ruler of the synagogue's house certain which said, Thy daughter is dead: why troublest thou the Master any further? As soon as Jesus heard the word that was spoken, he saith unto the ruler of the synagogue, Be not afraid, only believe." (Mark 5:22, 23, 35–43; Luke 7:12–15)

In this Scripture Jairus must have heard of Jesus, and the miracles He had done also, because *he made a faith confession* after he humbled himself at Jesus feet by saying: "come lay thy hands on her, that she may be healed; and she shall live." He

---

[20]   NKJV foot.: *Rebuked ... sea* demonstrates Jesus' authoritative reign over the entire earth, including inclement elements that might find their source in the destructive power of the Evil One.

was desperate, but expecting a miracle that he *believed* Jesus could do. Then the situation got worse, and he heard bad news that probably really shook him. *But as soon as Jesus heard it,* He encouraged Jairus to not be afraid, *Only Believe!*

The Amplified says: "Overhearing but ignoring what they said, Jesus said to the ruler of the synagogue, Do not be seized with alarm and struck with fear; only keep on believing." The NLV adds: "and she will be made well." He was saying don't let any fearful thoughts in, to rob you of your faith in Me. Keep trusting. It's not over yet, all things are possible when you *believe*!

Then they went to the house where the mourners already had her buried, but Jesus said, "Why make ye this ado, and weep? The damsel is not dead, but sleepeth." (v. 39) Jesus then took control of the circumstances calmly, and *spoke to the girl* when He took her by the hand, and immediately the girl arose and walked, proving she was alive! So sometimes *walking in faith, speaking words of faith, making a faith command* and *touching* are all involved in the healing process.

In all three stories: Jairus, the woman with the issue of blood and the Centurion, *didn't say anything else after they spoke their faith,* which can make or break your deliverance or miracle. Their obedience brought them the miracles they *believed* for with Jesus help.

Jesus said to Martha before He raised Lazarus from the dead, if you would *believe* you would see the glory of God! (John 11:40) So our part is to believe, say and receive our miracle; then don't let the enemy rob you of it—hang on to it like a Bull dog! A mighty woman of God said in an article I read recently to say: "**I won't stop praying and believing until I get my miracle!**"

When wondering whether it is God's will to heal, notice in all these Scriptures, Jesus never turned anyone away that needed healing. He never put sickness on anyone, or said they needed to keep it a little while longer to learn a lesson. That is not His nature, and doesn't agree with the Word that says He came to destroy the works of the devil, and give us life more abundantly! (1 John 3:8b; John 10:10)

Because "God anointed Jesus of Nazareth with the Holy Ghost and with power: who went about doing good, and healing all that were oppressed [21]of the devil; for God was with him" (Acts 10:38). NKJV confirms that it was God's will *to use Jesus to do good and heal all that were* "oppressed of the devil", for God was with Him. "Every good gift and every perfect gift is from above, and cometh down from the Father of lights, with whom is no variableness, neither shadow of turning" (James 1:17). So if it's not good, it's not from God, and He is unchanging about this, so get rid of it!

When a country or person is treated this way, the reason is *the oppression of the devil*, and they need God's help to deliver them through Jesus (1John 3:8). So cry out to Jesus to come to your situation or country and make it whole—*peaceful.*

Your confession could be: "Jesus, fulfill Your purpose to destroy the works of the devil in this country and our lives, so that we may have and enjoy life, and have it in abundance to the

---

[21]   *oppress*: suppress--To crush or burden by abuse of power or authority, to burden spiritually or mentally, . . . weigh heavily upon. *Merriam-Webster Inc*

full, till it overflows. And, that we may do all that You've called us to do, which is help and support others to spread the Gospel."

Authority over things that can be seen: In *Mark 11:21–24, Jesus taught His disciples after He spoke to the fruitless fig tree: "Jesus answering saith unto them, Have faith in God", which is a very important factor in this teaching of how to handle a problem in your life. Without *faith in God* that He hears you, you've got nothing! Remember "without faith it is impossible to please Him: for he that cometh to God must believe that He is, and that He is a rewarder of them that diligently seek him."

That's how Jesus got His prayers answered. He said: "Father, I thank You that You have heard me and I know You always hear me" (John 11:41, 42 NKJV). His confidence as a son of God, should be our confidence also, as we are sons of God. "For you are all sons of God through faith in Christ Jesus" (Gal. 3:26 NKJV).

When Jesus cursed the fig tree in Mark 11:19, He was specific about what He wanted to happen to it, so He spoke it out, and He expected His words to be fulfilled. His faith command got results, "And presently the fig tree withered away." It must have been like watching one of those speeded up scenes on TV of something shriveling up and dying, because the verse says that *the disciples marveled.* (Matt. 21:20)

The keys to having your prayers answered are: (1) faith in God, not doubting; (2) saying or commanding the mountain or problem to be cast into the sea, and (3) *believing* it will be done, because He said it would. Now read this over again and meditate on it. Learn that verse*, so you can use it in your life and circumstances: the what-so-evers that need to be changed.

If you obeyed this Scripture, and *believed that you received* whatsoever things you desired, then YOU HAVE them, because you *believe* He heard you when you prayed. (He promises to never leave you nor forsake you. Heb. 13:5b) Next do what Jesus did before He called Lazarus out of the tomb, and *thank God that He has heard you*, because you *believe* He did. (John 11:41)

First John 5:14,15: "This is the confidence that we have in him, that, if we ask anything according to his will, he heareth us: and if we know that he hear us, whatsoever we ask, we know that we have the petitions that we desire of him." So thank Him and praise Him!

Jerry Savelle said in one of his teachings that "It's *the depth of your praise* that determines the outcome." Then everyone in his audience begins shouting praises to God all at the same time. That's faith, because they *believed* they received their answers, which pleases God and causes Him to act.

> According to your faith be it unto you.
> —Matthew 9:29

Next *believe* He is able to do anything—He is The Creator of all things. Then *believe He is willing to give you the desires of your heart*, because He loves you, so don't cast away your confidence, which hath great recompence of reward (Heb. 10:35), and *keep praising!* Here you have to stand praising in faith—*steadfast, unwavering*—even if nothing has changed. Because *it is only faith when we believe no matter what*, leaning totally on God's Word.

Now guys praising isn't just for women. Have you noticed that almost all band and worship leaders are men? So be the man after God's own heart in your family, and lead them in worshiping the Lord each day, especially at church. You'll be doubly blessed by Him, and an excellent example to your family as a godly leader.

Now your part is to *make a faith command* regarding the mountain (Matt. 17:20), or problem, to cause it to move and be cast into the sea—from here to there—away—out of here! So you have to say it, not just think it, *without doubting in your heart* that it can happen! Then *believe* it will, before you have it.

You must BELIEVE YOU RECEIVE IT, BEFORE YOU HAVE IT!

A mighty man of God used to say: "Doubt and do without; with faith believe and receive. Expect a miracle!" He also said: **"Something good is going to happen to you today!"** This is confirmed by Psalms 68:19: "Blessed be the Lord, who daily loadeth us with benefits, even the God of our salvation! Selah" [AB: pause, and calmly think about that]!

Confession brings possession! Jesus said, "Blessed are they that have not seen and yet have believed" (John 20:29b). Don't be a "doubting Thomas" that said he had to see it first to believe. You don't need to *believe* when you are seeing it!

Believing is acting as if what you're believing for is true— *you have it—you own it, that it is yours!* So now it's your part to take action, because you have believed. So thank God for it— that's really *believing!*

This goes back to what Jesus said: "Have faith in God, because he who believes on Him will by no means be put to shame" (1Pet. 2:6a). And I would add: *Praise Him* and *praise*

Him every time you think of it, until you have it or see it. Then of course, give Him glory for it.

> Let my mouth be filled with Your praise and
> with Your glory all the day.
> —Psalms 71:8 NKJV

Matthew 9:35–10:1:

> And Jesus went about all the cities and villages, teaching in their synagogues, and preaching the gospel of the kingdom, and healing every sickness and every disease among the people. But when He saw the multitudes, He was moved with compassion on them, because they fainted, and were scattered abroad, as sheep having no shepherd. Then saith he unto His disciples, The harvest truly is plenteous, but the laborers are few. Pray ye therefore the Lord of the harvest that he will send forth laborers into His harvest. And when He had called unto him His twelve disciples, He gave them power against unclean spirits, to cast them out, and to heal all manner of sickness and all manner of disease.

This Scripture has been prayed to bring in laborers to get people "saved", but it doesn't say anything about getting people saved. It is talking about people being delivered and healed, by exercising authority over unclean spirits, casting them out, and then healing all kinds of sickness and disease in their bodies. Jesus is saying we need more anointed disciples with authority to help Me, so pray for more *Believers that will exercise the authority given to them.*

Generally, people are so grateful to be healed that they are then open to receive the Savior. One minister used to say that "Healing is the dinner bell for Salvation." That's why we need more healing seminars.

As you meditate on these Scriptures, get in line to receive your healing just as the others did. **Believe He is healing you as you read these words**. He is the Word. "And the Word became came flesh and dwelt among us." (John 1:14) He was *manifested*—visible to their sight. Yes!

Picture Jesus in front of you (visible) touching you where you need healing, and praise Him, or give Him glory, as the others did that received their healing. Then continue to stand praising Him until your healing is *manifested. Pain does not change God's Word,* so keep focused and praise Him!

> In all these things we are *more than conquerors*
> through him that loved us.
> —Romans 8:37 (Emphasis added)

There have been testimonies for years of people seeing Jesus in these days in dreams, visions and in front of them in various countries and situations. This fulfills the Scripture that says, "I was found by those who did not seek Me; I was made manifest to those who did not ask for Me" (Rom. 10:20 NKJV).

Generally these manifestations have caused people to receive Him as Lord, tell others and change whole villages! His manifestation brought wonderful fruit, as when Jesus got Saul's attention on the road to Damascus and stopped his plan to destroy more disciples of the Way (which Jesus ministry was called at the beginning), even though he had permission to do it. (Acts 9:1–9) Another verse that proves Jesus is the same yesterday, today and forever.

Heals man with withered hand: "Then He saith to the man, Stretch forth thine hand. And he stretched it forth; and it was restored whole, like as the other" (Matt. 12:13). The man's obedience brought him a healthy hand, as he stretched it out at Jesus command.

> The blind receive their sight, and lame walk;
> the lepers are cleansed and the deaf hear;
> the dead are raised up and
> the poor have the gospel preached to them.
> —Matthew 11:5

"Then was brought unto Him one possessed with a devil, blind[22] and dumb; and He healed him, insomuch that the blind and dumb man both spake and saw" (Matt. 12:22). Jesus healed two areas of this man [even though he was demon-possessed] at the same time, which were vital to his existence. His whole life was changed for the better, because of God's love. *Nothing is impossible!*

Even the woman with "the spirit of infirmity" for eighteen *years* was *loosed* from her infirmity, when Jesus spoke to her and laid His hands on her. (Luke 13:12, 13) She was *immediately* made straight and glorified God. Jesus also *restored* the man who had an infirmity thirty-eight *years* at the Pool of Bethesda

---

[22] Demons bring upon people evils as blindness, and take possession of them. *The Handy Bible Dictionary & Concordance*

(John 5:9) when *He spoke to him*, and *immediately* the man was healed. [I love that word 'immediately!']

For He said, "But the Father Who lives continually in Me does (His) works (His own miracles, deeds of power)" (John 14:10 AB). God's will "was to undo (destroy, loosen, and dissolve) the works of the devil has done." by sending Jesus. (1 John 3:8 AB)

So the devil: the *deceiver*[23] can then make you *feel* like you have something in your body you don't actually have. *It's a deception*! He is a liar and thief: one who steals your peace, money, health and anything else he can get away with, if you let him; but Jesus cut him off, and rebuked him from those who needed something good, or healing, because He came to give us life abundantly.

Did you know that **God loves you so much** that He has given you more than a "just get by life"? In fact He says in Philippians 4:19: "But my God shall supply all your need according to His riches in glory *by Christ Jesus*." Now if you are wealthy, but have a disease, wouldn't your *need* be health? Yes, of course it would. Money or titles don't do anyone any good when they are dying of a disease. They need the Healer—Jesus! Just as in the story of Jairus (one of the synagogue's rulers), whose daughter was dying, Jesus healed her when Jairus *came in faith and humbled himself before* Jesus in Mark 5:22, 23, 35–43, Matt. 9:18, 19, 23–26.

And, at the same time, Jesus healed the woman with the issue of blood (for twelve years), who had spent all that she had and was no better, but rather grew worse. But *she pressed through* the crowd (as an unclean woman, with the ruler of

---

[23] to act or practice of deceiving: deception . . .trick. *Merriam-Webster Inc*

the synagogue nearby) with her *confession of faith in Jesus on her lips*: "For she said, If I may touch but His clothes, I shall be whole. And straightway the fountain of her blood was dried up; and she felt in her body that she was healed of that plague . . . And when the woman saw that she was not hid, she came trembling; and falling down before Him, she declared unto Him before all the people for what cause she had touched Him and how she was healed immediately. And He said unto her, Daughter, be of good comfort: thy faith had made thee whole; go in peace." (Luke 8:43–48)

Matthew's account says in 9:21 AB: "For she kept saying to herself, If only I may touch His garment, I shall be restored to health." So this is an example of *continual faith confessions* bringing the blessing we desire. Matthew 9:20–23 says, she "was made well from that hour!" Hallelujah! So some healings are immediate and some come within the *hour, or begin at the time of *believing*. (*See John 4:51–53 also)

In these Scriptures, even though the devil caused trouble, disease or death, Jesus took it: "He Himself took our infirmities and bore our sicknesses" (Matt. 8:17). Notice it says "He Himself", the spotless Lamb of God. God didn't assign this job to anyone else. No one could have fulfilled *the Blood sacrifice that was needed*, but God's perfect Son—God, in the form of man—**Jesus**! (John 1:1)

The above Scripture refers to Isaiah 53:2–12 (vv. 4, 5 AB), "Surely He has borne our griefs (sicknesses, weaknesses, and distresses) and carried our sorrows and pains [of punishment], yet we [ignorantly] considered Him stricken, smitten, and afflicted by God [as if with leprosy]." Leprosy was a term used for any skin disease like leprosy at that time. You could confess this

Scripture that "**Jesus was afflicted with** _____ **for me!**"

No distance with Spirit: In the story of the woman from Canaan, (Matt. 15: 22, 28) who came to get deliverance for her daughter at home, Jesus located her faith in Him, and said to her: "O woman, great is thy faith: be it unto thee even as thou wilt. And her daughter was made whole from that very hour." So even though the daughter was in another location, Jesus delivered her at that very hour *by His Spirit!*

Notice He didn't say anything or shout. He just complimented the woman on her faith, and then said to her: "Let it be to you as you desire." (NKJV: deliverance of the demon-possession of her daughter.) Nothing is too hard for the Lord! The Centurion's servant was also *healed at another location,* when he asked Jesus to just speak a word. (Luke 7:2, 3)

Evidence of God's love: "And Jesus went forth, and saw a great multitude; and was moved with compassion toward them, and healed their sick (Matt. 14:14). Compassion is the direct motive for at least five of Jesus' miracles. So believe in His compassion for you!

Touching His garment heals: "And when the men of that place had knowledge of Him, they sent out into all that country round about, and brought unto Him all that were diseased, and besought Him that they might only touch the hem of His garment: and as many as touched were made perfectly whole" (Matt. 14:35, 36). Had they heard about the woman that had been healed by touching it also?

Luke 6:17–19 gives more detail of possibly the same situation or a similar one: "A great multitude of people from all Judea and Jerusalem, and from the seacoast of Tyre and

Sidon, who came to hear Him, and be healed of their diseases; and they that were vexed with unclean spirits: and they were healed. And the whole multitude sought to touch Him: for there went *virtue out of Him and healed them all."

Notice people who heard of Him, came and asked if they could touch his garment—showing respect. Next they were *willing to be taught*; they *believed* and *expected to receive* their healing or deliverance if they could but touch Him. Those that did, *received* what they expected: the *power* from Him to be healed.

"And great multitudes came unto Him, having with them those that were lame, blind, dumb, maimed, and many others; and cast them down at Jesus' feet, and He healed them. Insomuch that the multitude wondered, when they saw the dumb to speak, the maimed to be whole, the lame to walk, and the blind to see: and they glorified the God of Israel" (Matt. 15:30, 31). No infirmity of any kind was impossible for Jesus to heal, and He said I do the will of my father.

Man with unclean spirit: "But Jesus rebuked him, saying, Be quiet (*lit. Be muzzled!) and come out of him!" Mark 1:25–27c NKJV: "For with authority He commands even the unclean spirits, and they obey Him."[24] In Luke 10:19 NKJV, Jesus said, "Behold, I give unto you power to tread on serpents and scorpions, and over all the power of the enemy, and nothing shall by any means hurt you."[25] Jesus has already defeated the

---

[24]   Foot: in Mark 1:23* NKJV says, Jesus accepted the reality of demons. In fact, Jesus used His authority over them as a sign that He had brought the kingdom of God near. Furthermore, He gave to His followers authority over evil spirits. See Luke 10:19, 2 Cor. 10:3

[25]   The footnote: Serpents and scorpions are symbols of spiritual enemies and demonic power, over which Jesus has given His follower's power.

enemy at the cross, but it's up to us to *stand our ground and* **enforce** all that Jesus bought and paid for us there! So do what Jesus would do, and resist the enemy and cast him into the abyss in Jesus' Name! (Luke 8:31)

I live by the faith of the Son of God
—Galatians 2:20d

Giving us authority over the enemy, etc. is actually the New Testament verse of the Old Testament verse Genesis 1: 27, 28: "So God created man in His own image; in the image of God created he him; male and female created he them. And God blessed them, and God said unto them, Be fruitful and multiply, and replenish the earth, and subdue it: and have dominion over the fish of the sea, and over the fowl of the air, and over every living thing that moveth upon the earth."

The footnote in NKJV: Dominion over . . . the earth: God created man to be His kingdom agent, to rule and subdue the rest of creation, including the aggressive satanic forces, which would soon infringe upon it. Also: "Man's ability to sustain his role as delegated ruler of Earth will rest in his continued obedience to God's rule as King of all. His power to reign in life will extend only as far as his faithfulness to obey God's law."—Jack W. Hayford, see contributors

While we are on this subject, be careful where you go, what you watch, and who you spend time with. Ephesians 6:12 talks about "the rulers of darkness of this age", which are evil, sinful, wicked, dismal, hidden or secret. Now that sounds like nothing but trouble and could be *the door opener* to misery, because there is nothing good about the evil—the devil. He is the arch-enemy of God and of man. He tries to frustrate God's plans and purposes for human beings. His principal method of attack is *by temptation.*[26]

I heard a minister share on his broadcast, that the guy that mowed people down on his shooting spree in the news at that time, had no reason to do it, except that he had spent a long time watching video games doing similar things.

So just because there is a new thriller at the theater, that tries to frighten you with real or created beings, don't go! That's nightmare material for you and your family! The devil would love to bring that junk back into your memory and torment you with it. If Jesus wouldn't watch it, why would you? That includes most of the sitcoms on TV, which lead you to believe "Everything is alright." *It's not, if it doesn't agree with the Word.*

Here is a description of Heaven: "But without are the dogs and those who practice sorceries (magic arts) and impurity [the lewd, adulterers] and the murderers and idolaters, and everyone who loves and deals in falsehood (untruth, error, deception, cheating)" (Rev. 22:15 AB).

And 21:27 AB adds: "But nothing that defiles or profanes or is unwashed shall ever enter it, nor anyone who commits abominations (unclean, detestable, morally repugnant things) or practices falsehood, but *only those whose names are recorded in Lamb's Book of Life.*" (Emphasis added) So fellowship with Believers, and pray for and witness with *the power of the Holy Spirit* for the others to be "saved".

---

[26]   *Vine's CE Dictionary* specifically says: he tempts man to do evil, Eph 4:27; he afflicts men with physical sufferings, Acts 10:38; he lays snares, 1Tim. 3:7.

> Let us therefore cast off the works of darkness,
> and let us put on the armourof light.
> —Romans 13: 12b

In Ray Comfort's (*The Way of the Master*) interviews of the people on the street for the new *NOAH and the last days* DVD they produced, he talks to people who said they were Christians, who watch R rated movies, live together (unmarried), had tattoos, etc. and were proud of it. Sounds like *they made up their own rules for life.* The others he talked to were Gay, atheists, or just didn't care. With the direct questions he always asks, I'm sure he gave them much to think about, when they moved on from their conversation with him.

> Not everyone that saith unto me, Lord, Lord, shall enter into the kingdom of heaven; but he that doeth the will of my Father which is in heaven. Many will say to me in that day, Lord, Lord, have we not prophesied in thy name? and in thy name have cast out devils? And in thy name done many wonderful works? And then will I profess unto them, I never knew you: depart from me, ye that work iniquity

> —Matthew 7:21, 22

In the story about the man or demoniac of the Gadarenes in Matthew. 8:28–34, demons entered the man, which changed the way he thought and acted, until Jesus cast them out into the pigs. Demons need a body to live in to do some of their dirty work on this earth; and unless you have the gift of Discerning of spirits (1 Cor.12:10), you can't tell if they are in a crowd of people *unless they act up.* Remember we have dominion over every living thing that moves about on the earth. (Gen. 1:28)

Not all people go to church *regularly, read the Bible daily, obey it and serve the Lord whole heartedly. So most people with a carnal, selfish nature can be passing by you every day when you are out and about. That's why it's God's will that you stay close to Him, your Savior, Protector, Shepherd, Deliverer and everything else. *Jesus is the Way, the Truth and the Life.* Amen! [*I recently read that people go to church an average of twice a month. The rest are out having breakfast, jogging, shopping, golfing, or working, etc. we've observed.]

The Censors of movies and TV are not Christian, and have become lax in their censorship of the programs most families watch, including the commercials. Don't receive everything they tell you. Most news people are _not_ Christians; why would you believe them? When you are mature enough in the Spirit, He will quicken you about what you are watching and make you feel uncomfortable, because we are to "abstain from all appearance of evil" (1 Thess. 5:22). So ask Him how you should spend your time. "Yet you do not have because you do not ask*"* (James 4:2). So ask!

What you watch and listen to affects your soul, will and emotions. It opens the door to the devil or to the Holy Spirit. It plants the seed of fear to worry, anxiety and anger. Before you know it, you are saying things out of your emotions or flesh you wish you hadn't, instead of out of a godly spirit, which was trained up in the things of the Lord that *God can agree with: wholeness, righteousness, truth, love,* etc. (2 Tim. 1:7; 1 Thess. 5:23)

Don't just accept every thought and run with it. Ask yourself: Why am I thinking that? If it doesn't agree with the

Word, *change it to agree*. That's why you need to read the Word to know what to think. Why listen to the radio if it is not Christian Broadcasting? The music and the opinions will plant seeds of trouble for your future, and change the way you think about things.

"Catch us the foxes, the little foxes that spoil the vines, for our vines have tender grapes" (Song of Solomon 2:15 NKJV). Notice it says "tender grapes"; *don't let your children watch that junk either.* It forms their thinking that if it's on TV, the movies, or Mom and Dad are watching it, it's OK. Do you want to deal with the problems that follow like disobedience, resistance to your authority, and hardness of heart to name a few? It also affects their work ethics when they get a job or go to college.

Failure to train your children can lead to greater ungodliness as in the families of Eli, Samuel, David, and King Solomon, plus all the other kings and leaders in the Old Testament.

Second Chronicles 27: 1–34:2, King Jotham *did what which was right* in the sight of the Lord, but his son *Ahaz did not.* Then Hezekiah *did that which was right*, and restored everything that had been let go regarding the service of the Lord, and much more; but his son Manasseh, "*did that which was evil* in the sight of the Lord, like unto the abominations of the heathen, whom the Lord had cast out before the children of Israel" (33:1–34) But his son Amon *did that which was evil*, even after his father had humbled himself before the Lord and changed his ways! Next Josiah at age eight! "*did that which was right* in the sight of the Lord, and walked in the ways of David his father, *and declined neither to the right hand, nor to the left.* He was fully committed.

This went on and on for years and years, and never does the Bible say that the king taught his son, who was next in line to the throne, which, of course, was the most important position in the whole country, and would determine who the people would follow: the king or the Lord.

When all the godly kings failed to train their sons, it affected the people that knew them, or the nation. Generally after a godly king straightened out God's people, and set them on the path to obey Him, all would revert back to disobedience after he died; *even after they fully followed the Lord for years!*

The people believed and followed the Lord when they saw the signs and wonders in the reign of the king, but went back to their idols when they were not taught to believe in Jehovah Jireh, Almighty God, Who could provide all their needs, and had done it for years.

During the reign of the good kings, they were so busy cleaning up and restoring the whole country back to following the Lord, that they neglected teaching their children. Are you so busy with your job, committees, extracurricular activities, etc. that you don't have time to spend teaching your children how to walk with the Lord? Children learn by example. What are they seeing in you that resembles Christ? Will they say I want to be just like my parents, because they followed the Lord? If not, read Romans 12 for some ideas of where to begin now to become that good example.

> Let your light so shine before men,
> that they may see your good works,
> and glorify your Father which is in heaven.
> —Matthew 5:16

Proverbs 22:6: "Train up a child in the way he should go: and when he is old, he will not depart from it." Notice there is no please or when you get around to it in this verse, because it is coming from the man God gave wisdom to. If you don't train your children in the ways of the Lord, they will learn from where they spend most of their time: good or bad. 'Bad company produces bad fruit.' Statistics show that most crimes are committed by children that don't have a strong, godly father at home to teach them right and wrong.

Just because a TV program or movie is animated, doesn't mean it's suitable for children to watch. There is a lot of junk that is animated on TV and at the theater. [I remember years ago going to a Disney movie: *Fantasia* with Mickey Mouse and a wizard that we walked out of, because it was loaded with demons and my spirit couldn't stand it!]

In Genesis 27: 27–29, 38–40; 48:14–16, Isaac blesses his children, and then Israel blesses Joseph's children with blessings regarding their future. I've read where the Jews continue to do this over their children, and that's why they are so successful in business, inventions, etc., even taking over twenty Nobel Prizes.

So begin speaking blessings over your children in all the areas of their lives, and do it on their birthdays, family gatherings, weddings, holidays, etc. There is no telling what this could do for them to bring about their healthy self-esteem, and affirmation of your love. You could even have it printed and framed to post in their room or home. If you want to be fancy, you could have it printed on a scroll through *Scrolls Unlimited, Inc.* in Mackinaw City, Michigan: www.scollsunlimited.com.

Also, a majority of movies and TV programs have to do with killing or adultery (fornication is the Bible term), instead of entertainment, which means: cheer, gladden, please, divert, amuse among others. While the antonym means: repulse, disgust, annoy and I might add creates <u>fear</u>, which is the worst way to spend your time, but the devil loves it. *If you are in fear, you have no faith—O.* "Without faith you are up a creek without a paddle." helpless, which is where the devil wants you.

"It's insanity to think things will change, if you don't make a change!" So begin today to change what you have been doing that has not brought any good fruit into your life, *to things that will bring blessings.* Choose today who you will *believe* and serve: the Lord or the devil!

> The fear of the Lord is the
> beginning of wisdom and
> the knowledge of the
> Holy One is understanding.
> —Proverbs 9:10 NKJV

Since it takes twenty-one days to create a new habit and break old ones, maybe it's time to begin watching Christian programming, going to *Dove*, or *Focus on the Family* approved movies, and concerts, etc. It's also a good time to pay attention to the ratings, and stay out of anything PG13 or worse. [Only *a little poison* in brownies will create a lot of misery, or kill you!]

Whatever you sow you reap (Gal.6:7). Keep the files of your mind clean—uncluttered with junk. It is written: "We have the mind of Christ" (1 Cor. 2:16). Say to yourself: "Would Jesus think that?" If we are reading enough of the Word, people should see it in our lives by the decisions we make, what we say and do. You may be the only Christian that your neighbors or the people that you work with know. If you were accused of being a Christian, would there be any evidence to convict you?

> Whether you eat or drink, or whatever you do,
> do all to the glory of God.
> 1 Corinthians 10:31 NKJV

Guys let's talk about those Bowl games that you watch with your friends or family. Just because businesses and commercials lead you to believe you need junk food and a lot of alcohol to enjoy them, doesn't mean you have to participate in their way of thinking. Junk food and alcohol create obesity, heart trouble, and Diabetes to name a few. The sugar (in alcohol, white flour, white potatoes, white rice, and pasta) in your body creates an *acid environment* which leads to Cancer, also. So don't lose your head, think rationally, instead of carnally.

> Know ye not that a little leaven leaveneth the whole lump?
> —1 Corinthians 5:6b[27]

> Who hath woe? who hath sorrow?
> who hath contentions?
> who hath babbling? who hath wounds without cause?
> who hath redness of eyes?
> They that tarry long at the wine; they
> that go to seek mixed wine.
> —Proverbs 23: 29, 30

---

[27] NKJV footnote: Leaven has a fermenting action that illustrates [the corrupting power of evil]. The yeast of sin can spread if unchecked. *Ignored discipline* denies the purpose of Christ's death.

Regarding "carnally", you are setting an example for your children and others, when you watch the half-time shows that have progressed to Las Vegas style entertainment. Each year they "push the envelope" about how far they will go to entertain the audience with skimpy outfits, suggestive actions and dances, besides the words in the songs they sing. What does that have to do with a football game?

> No temptation has overtaken you
> except such as is common to man;
> but God is faithful, who will not allow you to be tempted
> beyond what you are able,
> but with the temptation will also make the way of escape,
> that you may be able to bear it.
> —1 Corinthians 10:13

How about some clean 'retro football' half-time entertainment *that the whole family can watch and enjoy together*, without being embarrassed by the carnal entertainers? A good confession would be: "**I will set no wicked thing before mine eyes**" (Ps. 101:3). Because, your inner life (spirit and soul), is effected by what you focus on for good or for bad.

> Put on the Lord Jesus Christ,
> and make no provision for the flesh, to fulfill its lusts.
> —Romans 13:14

Think about it: King Herod had John the Baptist's head cut off after watching Salome dance before him, then he offered her anything in his kingdom as a reward. Could *the lust of the eyes* have made him irrational to offer such a reward?

119

Did I forget to tell you one day you will have to stand before the Lord and explain your actions while here on earth? How you spent your leisure time is probably on the list of questions? *Practice disciplining yourself now*, so you will be ready for that day.

BLESSED is every one that feareth the Lord;
that walketh in his ways.
—Psalm 128:1

* * *

A Deaf-Mute Healed: "And He took him aside from the multitude, and put His fingers into his ears, and He spit and touched his tongue; and looking up to heaven, He sighed, and saith unto him, Ephphtha, that is, Be opened. And straightway his ears were opened, and the string of his tongue was loosed, and he spake plain" (Mark 7:33–35). The words of Jesus can fix and make whole!

Blind Man Healed at Bethsaida: "And He took the blind man by the hand, and led him out of the town; and when He had spit on his eyes and put His hands upon him, He asked him if he saw ought. And he looked up and said, I see men like trees, walking. After that He put His hands again upon his eyes, and made him look up: and he was restored and saw every man clearly" (Mark 8:23–25)[28] [I have used this verse many times, when I have prayed for people that did not receive their healing the first time they were prayed for.]

---

[28] The NKJV footnote says: This healing is unique in that it is accomplished in stages.

A Boy Healed: "When Jesus saw that the people came running together, He rebuked the foul spirit, saying unto him, Thou dumb and deaf spirit, I charge thee, come out of him and enter no more into him." (Mark 9:17–27) Because of the boy's symptoms and actions, Jesus *named the spirit* that he needed to be delivered of, exercised his authority to cast it out, *and forbid it to come back to him.* He knew the enemy immediately comes to steal, kill and destroy (John 10:10a), so he took care of the boy's future also. Be sure when you do this to say: "**Enter him or me no more!** Or: **I forbid it to come back in Jesus' Name!**"

Here Jesus exercises the "discerning of spirits"[29] gift as spoken of in 1 Corinthians 12:10. This is important in *judging a situation*, so you know how to pray or take authority over it, as the Holy Spirit leads. Sometimes this must be done quickly, *so hearing from the Holy Spirit is vital!* to change the circumstances for the better or peace.

Jesus Heals Blind Bartimaeus, Mark 10:46–52:

> And they came to Jericho: and as he went out of Jericho with His disciples and a great number of people, blind Bartimaeus, the son of Timaeus, sat by the highway side begging. And when he heard that it was Jesus of Nazareth, he began to cry out, and say, Jesus, thou Son of David, have mercy on me. And many charged him that he should hold his peace: but he cried the more a great deal, Thou Son of David,

---

[29] NKJV footnote: *Discerning of spirits* is the ability to discern the spirit world, and especially to detect the true source of circumstances or motives of people.

have mercy on me. And Jesus stood still, and commanded him to be called. And they call the blind man saying unto him, Be of good comfort, rise; he calleth thee. And he, casting away his garment, rose, and came to Jesus. And Jesus answered and said unto him, What wilt thou that I should do unto thee? The blind man said unto Him, Lord, that I might receive my sight. And Jesus said unto him, Go thy way; thy faith hath made thee whole. And immediately he received his sight, and followed Jesus in the way.

Since the biggest characteristic of God is His Mercy, it stopped Jesus when He heard Bartimaeus cry out for it, which caused many to be healed in Jesus ministry at other times, because God is "plenteous in mercy unto all them that call upon thee" (Ps. 86:5). "It is of the Lord's mercies that we are not consumed, because his compassions fail not. They are new every morning: great is thy faithfulness" (Lam. 3:22, 23). So cry out for mercy, and expect to receive your miracle as he and others did.

$\mathcal{M}y$ $\mathcal{T}estimony$:

$\mathcal{H}ealed$ of $\mathcal{C}ancer,$
$\mathcal{D}elivered$ of $\mathcal{C}hemo\text{-}\mathcal{T}herapy$ and $\mathcal{D}epression!$

In the late summer of 1987, I made an appointment with my Gynecologist for a checkup. (I discovered later that I hadn't seen him for several years.) Prior to this I had been having digestive problems, so I saw a doctor, who told me I had a slow digestion. Not being satisfied with that diagnosis, I began treating myself by eliminating wheat, using digestive enzymes, etc., but those methods didn't help—I still had a protruding abdomen. Since I always had a tummy, I didn't get concerned about this except when I'd roll over in bed at night, and I felt like I was lying on a ball.

At that time, I was already a Spirit-filled Christian, trained up in the things of the Lord, like prayer, faith and the "laying on of hands". In fact, I was going regularly to Rev. Joan Hart's Bible studies and seminars.

I met Rev. Hart at Bible Study Fellowship in 1985, where we were one of many small groups of women, which met each Tuesday morning at a local church. From what I had learned from the Bible and her teaching, people could be healed through *prayer and the Word*, so I talked to her about my concern. After that she prayed for me to be healed of digestive problems *or* whatever else was wrong, but there was no major improvement.

With the pressure of my mother, husband and Rev. Hart, I made an appointment with Dr. Peake, GPYN, while still *believing* God to heal me.

I told him why I had come, and then had a routine checkup. Lying on my back made the ball in my abdomen quite obvious. He felt it and talked to me about women having fibrous masses, which were not generally serious; but he recommended that it be removed. He did mention that there was a possibility that it could be Cancer.

As I drove home, many thoughts went through my mind (and I'm very positive person), but by the time I called my husband, I was in tears, and he was sympathetic. I didn't want to have surgery. I didn't believe that was God's way. I *believed* when you were prayed for and hands were laid on you, the Lord healed!

My surgery was scheduled for right after Labor Day though, so that meant a *long weekend.* We went to my parent's home at a nearby lake, and got ready for my surgery, by making a new purple and white print caftan, and trying to make the best of it (I wanted to at least look good while I was in the hospital.)

As each day went by, it seemed my abdomen got larger (which was probably the deception of the devil), and made me glad something was going to be done, but I was still believing for my healing! I even talked about it as I was wheeled into the operating room: that I was still *believing* for my healing. I TOTALLY EXPECTED AT ANY SECOND the bump would disappear (other people have had miracles like that), and I wouldn't need the surgery, but I went to sleep instead.

When I woke up in my room, I felt as if there was a bonfire in my abdomen, which caused a *tremendous amount of PAIN!!!!*

Of course, they made me get up out of bed the first day, which added insult to injury. That is PAIN with a capital P!! I remember the pain medication didn't do enough, and never was on time, but, I recovered quickly. Each day I seemed to be noticeably better by evening than I was in the morning.

As soon as I could function, Dr. Peake began to discuss with me my surgery and condition. As it turned out, when he opened my abdomen, he had to remove a melon sized mass, which I believed was an exaggeration. He found that I had Ovarian Cancer in the second stage. He removed all of my female organs and rinsed out the area, to make sure it was clean of all Cancer. He believed he got it all, but recommended that I see an Oncologist right away to schedule Chemo-therapy.

Lee, my parents, our pastor and Rev. Hart were given all the details, which they did not concern me with until later. Rev. Hart kept the rest of the ministry informed, so they could be praying for the circumstances, me, my family and the doctors. I'm sure that's why I healed so fast.

I knew God was in control when the *Christian lady* that I shared my room with at the hospital was named *Grace*, and the Oncologist's name was <u>Dr. Lord</u>, also a Christian. He counseled us on the importance of Chemo-therapy, and recommended we start as soon as I felt well enough.

I had only heard of Chemo-therapy, but didn't know what it entailed. It required that my blood be tested frequently at the hospital; then I was admitted for an overnight stay to begin pumping the chemicals into my blood stream. Did you know that *Chemo-therapy cannot discern which cells are good or bad?* That's why it is not the best way to deal with Cancer.

This became very difficult to face each time I had to go back to the hospital, because I would go in feeling pretty good and leave feeling *terrible*! God's grace was there, however, because I think I ended up with only a total of three treatments from October to January.

Since one of the side effects is hair loss, the registered nurse (whose last name was <u>Christ</u>) offered me an ice-pack-type hat that was put on while the Chemo was being administered intravenously. I can still remember the *intense* discomfort. I don't know if it worked at all or just delayed my hair loss, but my hair fell out each time I washed it.

Picture this: no tummy, thin hair and sick, nauseous, can't eat. Life was miserable!

Each time I went for my treatment, the doctor tried something else, because my system reacted so badly. One time I felt like climbing the walls with anxiety symptoms, as a reaction to the Chemo. Besides that, my mouth reacted in *severe* Canker sores, which are hard to get rid of when you're healthy. Dr. Lord said he had never had anybody that had such a hard time with the drugs. Well, I never took drugs, besides that I learned about the healing that Jesus had provided for us through the cross.

By the time I was well enough, it was time for another treatment. I dreaded going into the hospital knowing I'd have to deal with misery when I'd leave. Now I was having problems with anxiety. That can make you sicker, and it did. I used to say "The cure is worse than the disease", which was a dumb confession.

During this time, I read my Bible and prayed Scriptures as I could. When you're suffering with the above symptoms, it's hard to read or do anything you should *to build up your faith.* Since I already had about six years of Bible study and teaching, I knew enough to keep me going in the right direction, and praise God for my friends that were lifting me up in prayer. Don't depend on this, however, because you are the only one who really knows what you need prayer for, besides they are busy with their own lives, which causes them to forget.

One day in October of 1987, Rev. Hart prayed for me, and *I believed I received my healing from Cancer.* She gave me a book to read by Norvel Hayes, called *Seven Ways Jesus Heals*, but I didn't read it until January 23, 1988, after I had the Marijuana Chemo-therapy, *which really made me sick!* In fact, all I could do was lie in my husband's Lazyboy chair and feel miserable. (That is not like me at all!)

That morning I got up for my time with the Lord, and picked up the book to read, *which was perfect timing.* I only read the first chapter on *Healing through FAITH*, and I got hooked. It was the story of blind Bartimaeus in Mark 10:46–52. Norvel had picked the story apart, explaining what happened to produce his miracle. First Bartimaeus heard that Jesus was coming, then he called out to Him *for mercy*, and He *continued to cry out for mercy, until he got Jesus' attention,* even though he was rebuked and told to be quiet, but *he was desperate.* He must have heard of the miracles Jesus did, and had FAITH for the miracle he needed.

Then Jesus stopped and called him; Bartimaeus *threw off his mantle in faith, sprang up and came to Jesus.* Jesus said to him, "What wilt thou that I should do unto thee?" Bartimaeus answered: "Lord, [making Jesus Lord] that I might receive my sight" [*asking the end result,* not healing.] "And Jesus said unto him, Go thy way; your Faith hath made thee whole. And immediately he received his sight, and followed Jesus in the way."

Believing I could do the same thing, I cried out to Jesus for mercy and *immediately I felt His POWER go down through me like a shower*. I received it as His healing touch, and began praising and praising Him! I was almost hysterical with excitement, praising and praising and praising Him with joy unspeakable!

Next I felt an urge to go to the bathroom, and when I turned around to flush the toilet, I noticed *foam all over the top of the water*, like the head on root beer—*confirmation of my deliverance of the Chemo-therapy!* That had never happened to me before or since, and that "sign" kept me for a long time.

Shortly after that, my husband woke up and came downstairs; he couldn't believe how different I was. I told him what had happened, but he was very cautious and concerned. When I shared the news with Rev. Hart, she said that she had been praying for me that morning.

That day, I cleaned and vacuumed the house, which would have been *an impossible thought* the day before! Next, I called Dr. Lord to cancel the next *five months* of Chemo-therapy that was scheduled. He did not like this idea, even after I excitedly told him what had happened. He told me about other women with Ovarian Cancer that tried to stand in faith and died. He shared how serious this type of Cancer was, and it was generally fatal, but I didn't budge. *I still believed what Jesus had done for me! He gave me evidence!*

> It is better to trust in the Lord
> than to put confidence in man.
> —Psalm 118:8

He finally relented, which disappointed my husband, and said I had to have a *CAT Scan*, and we set the date. I had the *CAT Scan* "in the name of Jesus", and awaited the results over a <u>very long weekend.</u>

Dr. Lord had some concern about liver damage, so had to get a full report, which took the extra days. My flesh waited *in agony* each hour until the next appointment. I think that was the longest weekend of my life, but when he came into the counseling room he said "I'm glad to say I was wrong." The final analysis was that I was clean! Thank you Jesus! You can imagine our rejoicing, even Dr. Lord! I almost ran out of the Oncology Clinic. I've never been back.

Sometime during this trial, I remember walking from the bathroom to our bedroom, as I was getting dressed for church on a Sunday morning, and hearing a verse from a Bible tape that was playing quickened my Spirit. The story is in Mark 5 about the woman with the issue of blood, and the verse was "she felt in her body that she was cleansed of the disease." Scripture confirmation is really nice, and I hung on to it for many years.

The devil was not done however.

My victory wasn't even comfy yet when Depression showed its ugly head. I couldn't stand the thought of Cancer. I didn't want to be around anybody that was going to talk about it in anyway, good or bad. Someone called me to encourage someone else that found out she had Cancer, but I couldn't talk to her. The fear of Cancer gripped me and caused Depression, which comes from the spirit of death and hell. *This is where I made a mistake and let fear in.* I should have cast it down and out at the beginning in Jesus' Name; then *confessed healing Scriptures daily, or more often,* to help me to stand on the Truth that *by His stripes I was healed!*

If you know anything about Depression, it's easy to get into, but hard to get out of. I cried, was sick to my stomach, feared everything, and tried to deal with it with sleep. Even though we were given free reservations to Boyne Mountain, a ski lodge in northern Michigan, I was so fearful of being away from home; we ended up going home early.

I found I did best when I worked hard, whether it was cleaning, gardening, or anything I could throw myself into.

Around that time, Rev. Hart was scheduled to have a women's retreat at *Miracle Camp* in South Western Michigan, on *Setting the Captives Free* (*Hart to Heart Ministries*). The whole retreat led up to a prayer that she had written from Scriptures, the Lord had given her. When we prayed this *Freedom Prayer,* which it was called, before we left on Saturday, *the spirit of Depression left!* I don't remember feeling anything; I was just "set free" from that nasty spirit. *I got my miracle!* but continued to pray that prayer for a long time after that.

Of course, my life went back to normal, and I've been telling my story to anyone that would listen, or who needed encouragement that **God still does miracles!** Thank you, Lord! I'm forever grateful!

Post script: Looking back on this, I believe the devil was trying to kill me, because he could see the Lord's hand on my life, and the damage I would cause him by sharing the Gospel, especially that Believers have authority over him *in Jesus' Name!*

* * *

Jesus Did the Will of God –

Jesus Forgives and Heals a Paralytic: When Jesus saw *the faith of men* bringing a paralytic through the roof, because there was no other way to get to Him while He was teaching (and the power or the Spirit of the Lord was present to heal), the man was healed. Luke 5:17–25 says, "And when He saw their faith, He said unto him, Man, thy sins are forgiven thee." Verse 23, 24: "Whether is easier, to say, Thy sins are forgiven thee; or to say, Rise up and walk? (He said unto the sick of the palsy) I say unto thee, Arise, take up thy couch, and go to thine house. And immediately he rose up before them, and took up that whereon he lay, and departed to his own house, glorifying God."

So the *faith and determination* of this man's friends *caused him to receive his miracle, when he couldn't do anything for himself.* Notice verse 23: Our Savior says the same thing to you, <u>you're just as saved and forgiven as you are healed</u>. Hallelujah!

Multitude healed: "And the whole multitude sought to touch Him for power went out from Him and healed them all" (Luke 6:19). Notice *healed them all*!

Heals Man with Dropsy: "And, behold, there was a certain man before him which had the dropsy. . . And He took him, and healed him, and let him go" (Luke 14:2, 4b). Dropsy is a swelling of the body caused by excess fluid in the tissues. Someone who has a problem retaining fluids might want to use this verse for deliverance of that malady such as: **"Father, as you healed the man with dropsy in the Bible, heal me of the curse of water retention in Jesus' Name."** Then *believe that He heard you,* so praise Him that it's no longer a problem in your life. From then on, praise Him anytime you think of it that you're delivered! You might even mark the day in your notes or on your calendar.

The Command for the Seventy Sent out: "And into whatsoever city ye enter, and they receive you, eat such things as are set before you: and heal the sick that are therein, and say to them, The kingdom of God is come nigh unto you" (Luke 10:9). NKJV note: The coming of God's kingdom and [the ministry of healing are not separated.] This ministry of healing is experienced throughout the whole of the Book of Acts, and in James 5:13–16 is declared as *one of the responsibilities of eldership in a local congregation.* (Emphasis added)

"The thief comes only in order to steal, and kill, and destroy. I came that they may have and enjoy life, and have it in abundance (to the full, till it overflows)" (John 10:10 AB) Here Jesus says the troublemaker: thief, another name for *the devil*, is the cause of misery in life, but Jesus came to give life more abundantly.[30] (John 10:10b)

Praise God that's good news, and we should tell others it's available to all that call upon the Name of the Lord and are saved! Because He has promised, I always expect abundance! *Poor people can't help others who need it.* We're blessed to be a blessing!

"And, behold, there was a woman which had a spirit of infirmity eighteen years, and was bowed together, and could in no wise lift up herself. And when Jesus saw her, He called her to Him, and said unto her, Woman, thou are loosed from thine infirmity. And He laid His hands on her: and immediately she

---

[30] NKJV Strong's #4053: Superabundance, excessive, overflowing, surplus, over and above, more than enough, profuse, extraordinary, above the ordinary, more than sufficient.

was made straight, and glorified God. Jesus said: "And ought not this woman, being a daughter of Abraham, whom Satan hath bound, lo, these eighteen years, be loosed from this bond on the Sabbath day?" (Luke 13:11–13,16)

<u>Refuse</u> to be dominated by any inherited diseases, or generational curses from your relatives in Jesus' Name! because you are born again, and all those diseases or curses were cancelled at that time when you *believed* and *received* Jesus as your Lord and Savior! Christians are redeemed from every curse written in the book of the law, and since the book of the law! (Gal. 3:13; Deu: 28:61)

Say this often "**I'm redeemed from all curses for Christ became a curse for me, that the blessings of Abraham may come upon me. It is written: No weapon (or curse) formed against me shall prosper!**" (Is. 54:17) Isn't a curse a weapon that tries to hurt or destroy you? It certainly makes you miserable, so it's a curse. *Speak the Word to get rid of it,* because the Word—Jesus— is living and powerful and sharper than any two-edged sword! (Heb. 4:12 NKJV) and God hastens to perform it. (Jer. 1:12) Revelation 1:16; 19:15 both talk about Jesus having a two-edged sword coming out of His mouth.

"And I will give you the keys[31] of the kingdom of heaven, and whatever you bind (declare to be improper and unlawful) on earth must be what is already bound in heaven, and what-ever you loose (declare lawful) on earth must be what is already

---

[31]   NKJV footnote: Keys denote authority. The Greek construction behind *will be bond* and *will be loosed* indicates that Jesus is the One who has activated the provisions through His cross; the church is then charged with implementation of what He has released through His life, death, and resurrection.

loosed in heaven" (Matt. 16:19 AB). Jesus is passing on to His church His authority or control *to bind* and *to loose* on earth.

Think about it, anything that is not in Heaven: misery, sickness, pain, disharmony, lack, homosexuality, lying, jealousy, envy, greed, pride, strife, selfishness, hatred, etc. *should not be on earth in your life!* **So bind, forbid, and declare them unlawful in your life in Jesus' Name!** Now **loose and declare lawful all that is in Heaven: health, peace, prosperity, harmony, joy, freedom from the enemy, security, and love into your life in Jesus' Name!** *Then praise God you have it now! Thank Him for it, and continue to thank Him for it. That's faith!*

> For I have come down from Heaven,
> not to do My own will,
> but the will of Him who sent Me.
> —John 6:38

Spiritual Gifts: Gifts of healings: Footnote for 1 Cor. 12:9 NKJV: Gifts of healings are those healings *that God performs supernaturally by the Spirit.* The plural suggests that as there are many sicknesses and diseases, the gift is related to healings of many disorders.

Chapter 8

Only Believe:
All Things are Possible

When I started reading my Bible one morning, I decided to follow the references for the Scripture Mark 10:26, 27 when the disciples asked Jesus, "Who then can be saved? He answered, "With men it is impossible, but not with God; for with God all things are possible."

This is one of my favorite scriptures, which I say to myself and others a lot; but this time, I marveled at how often *God said it in His Word*. In fact, eighteen times in some form! Do you think He's trying to tell us something?

Let me share some of the others, and the variety of circumstances where they were used. In Genesis 18:14, the Word says: "Is anything too hard for the Lord?" This is where the Lord is talking to Abraham about Sarah having a child in her old age. When He hears her laugh (from her tent), He made that statement convicting her of her unbelief.

When the people complained (Num.11:21–23) they didn't have meat to eat, and Moses went to the Lord to tell Him how many people–600,000–needed to be fed, "And the Lord said unto Moses, Is the Lord's hand waxed short? thou shalt see now whether My word shall come to pass unto thee or not." Then He sent lots of quail to hover over the ground, so they could reach them and gather them in. *At that same time*, He "took the Spirit that was on Moses and placed the same upon the seventy elders (v. 25) and they prophesied!"[32] He gave the people physical and spiritual food.

Another instance is when the Lord answers Job, after He describes what He had done without Job's help, "I know that thou canst do everything, and that no thought can be withholden from thee." (Job 42:2) Those are the words of a Believer!

In Isaiah 58:1 NKJV, after talking about the "Fasting that pleases God", Isaiah says: "Behold, the Lord's hand is not shortened that it cannot save; neither His ear heavy, that it cannot hear." It's because of their sins that He would not hear them, *not because He is not able.*

Another one in Isaiah 50:2c, "Is My hand shortened at all, that it cannot redeem? or have I no power to deliver?" He is asking why He hadn't been sought for Israel's answer. That's like when we try to do things ourselves, *instead of seeking God first.*

As Jeremiah (32:17) is worshiping the Lord (while Jerusalem was under siege from the king of Babylon) and asking why he should buy the field, he says: "Ah Lord God! behold, thou hast made the heaven and the earth by thy great power and stretched out arm, and there is nothing too hard for thee." Then God answers later in verse 27: "Behold, I am the Lord, the God of all flesh: is there any thing too hard for me?" Here again God is talking about His power to handle the situation at that time.

---

[32] The column reference says about v: 23 NKJV: Is the Lord's power limited?

In Luke 1:37, the angel said to Mary about Elizabeth, (a barren woman in her old age), that she would conceive a son, "For with God nothing shall be impossible." The angel knew it was not impossible, because Sarah had already had Isaac many generations before while in her nineties! Did you notice the angel even covered the future with "shall" be impossible. Doesn't that give you comfort for your circumstances?

As you can see, *nothing, no thing is impossible with God!* The impossible has already been done: Jesus being seen alive by over 500 people after He died on the cross, miracles, gang leaders and satanists turned into Evangelists, besides people being raised from the dead by *Believers*. His Word says it over and over again also. His Word describes in some detail how He turned the situation around for good, His will, in answer to prayer and faith, *or* to bless His children.

We have faced and *gone through* "impossible situations" in our own life, with God's help.

- ❖ *Time limits* were no problem for Him—He stretched them, or wasn't late!
- ❖ *Lack of money*—He provided, or showed us a better way.
- ❖ *Nowhere to move*—He opened our eyes to the way.
- ❖ *Sickness and disease*—He was my Deliverer and Healer.

He sent the *help* when we asked, and *peace* came when we trusted in Him. He gave us wisdom or direction in the Word, and by His Spirit. His LOVE was there in many ways, and I'm sure in ways we didn't even know about.

He has taken us from debt and lack to abundance and beauty; from Cancer and Chemo-therapy to health and energy; from Depression to joy and life. He has taken Lee and me from times of disunity to unity, from sorrow to Grace, and I believe He's told me the "Best is yet to come!"

Do you have a Red Sea to cross? Are your children disobedient? Does your future look grim? Do you need to do something you've never done before? Have you been waiting for a baby? Well, <u>trust God</u>!

Nothing is Impossible with Him!

Jesus said with faith during his time of greatest sorrow, in the garden of Gethsemane "Abba Father, all things are possible unto thee;" because He knew His father. (Mark 14:36) As children of God, we can ask Him for anything according to His Word—*His will*. I've done it over and over again, and He's answered!

Only Believe!

For more stories of God's rescue, read the miracles done by God's servants Elijah and Elisha in First and Second Kings. Or about Adonijah, who presumed himself king, yet Solomon was anointed in time, with pomp and rejoicing.

In the New Testament, Acts 9:21, 22 Saul, the church's greatest opponent, became her greatest advocate. In Acts 9:36–43 Dorcas, who was dead, washed and laid in an upper room, *then* Peter was sent for *in another town*, came to Joppa, went to the room, dealt with the people there, then prayed and the Lord raised her up! He is an awesome God! Hallelujah!

Chapter 9

Only Believe:
The Blood of Jesus!

Physical afflictions refer to the atoning work on the Cross, which is an accomplished fact: "By His *wounds you have been healed" (I Pet. 2:24 AB). Past tense! *Wounds* as a verb mean: to injure by tearing, cutting, or piercing the skin. *Affliction* means a state of distress or acute pain of the body or mind. The meaning of *wounds* is a perfect description of what happened when Pilot sent Jesus to be scourged; and *afflictions* are what He took of ours on Himself, when he suffered and died that first Good Friday.

Matthew 8:17b: "He Himself took our infirmities, and bore our sicknesses." Another version says, "He took on Himself our sicknesses and carried away our diseases." This refers to Isaiah 53:4, 5AB: "Surely He has borne our griefs (sicknesses, weaknesses, and distresses) and carried our sorrows and pains; Yet we considered Him stricken, smitten and afflicted by God [as if with leprosy.] But He was wounded (*pierced through) for our transgressions, He was bruised (*crushed) for our guilt and iniquities; the chastisement [needful to obtain] peace and well-being for us was upon Him, and with the stripes [that wounded] Him we are healed *and* made whole!" (*Emphasis added)

The synonym for *sickness* is illness, unsoundness. For *disease* it is ailment . . ., complaint . . ., disorder . . ., illness . . ., infirmity. ., malady . . ., sickness.[33] So sickness, disease, illness, and infirmity are interchangeable, and they all cause misery, which are all curses Jesus took from us, because He loves us.

This is looking *to the cross*, which is a "prophetic perfect" as in Romans 4:17 AB: "Who gives life to the dead and speaks of the nonexistent things that [He has foretold and promised] as if they [already] existed." Such as when you say: "**Thank You Lord it's so good to be healed!**"

"But thanks be to God, who gives us the victory through our Lord Jesus Christ!" (1 Cor. 15:57) Also in Revelation 12:11: "And they overcame him [the accuser of the brethren] by the Blood of the Lamb, and by the word of their testimony".[34] [I claim this a lot, because I believe in the power of the blood of the Lamb and the authority of God's Word—Jesus!]

Power of the Blood

*I read a testimony years ago about the power of the Blood
that saved a minister's family from rabid
foxes when he wasn't even there.
The story goes that there had been
reports of rabid foxes in the area
around this minister's property, so he
gathered some Believers to pray*

---

[33] *Merriam-Webster Inc*

[34] The footnote NKJV says: The church's constant posture under the authority of the Cross's victory by the blood of the Lamb and steadfastness to the promise and the authority of God's Word–the word of their testimony–is the key to their overcoming.

> *and <u>agree for the protection of the Blood</u>*
> *<u>of Jesus</u> around his property line.*
> *Then he left on a trip, and was contacted*
> *shortly after that by a friend,*
> *who had gone out to his property and found*
> *dead foxes along the property line.*
> *He took them to be tested, and discovered*
> *that they indeed were rabid!*

* * *

This relates to the Scriptures in Exodus 12:7 NKJV when God told Moses to tell the people "And they shall take of the blood and strike it on the two side posts and on the upper door post of the houses, wherein they shall eat it." Verse 13: "And the blood shall be a token upon the houses where ye are: and when I see the blood, I will pass over you; and the plague shall not be upon you to destroy you, when I smite the land of Egypt." Verse 23d: "And will not suffer the destroyer to come in unto your houses to smite you."

So since the blood of the lamb *protected* the Israelites after it was put on the outside of their doorways, why not do the same thing *by faith with the Blood of Jesus* over your doorways and bodies, to protect you from the enemy's attacks of sickness, disease, or misery of any kind? Isn't He your Savior?

You might say *in faith* as you touch that area of your doorways: **"I put the Blood of Jesus over the lintel and doorposts of our house that the enemy may not come in to kill, steal or destroy in Jesus' Name!"** Then trust that it is done, and you have the same protection that the children of Israel had from the destroyer.

Have Faith in the Blood!

Faith in the precious Blood of Jesus changes things for better health and life. *It is powerful!* When you are experiencing painful symptoms, confess the *Blood of Jesus* as you lay hands on that area of your body, until your body is back to normal. *Say it over and over again in faith.* It is miracle working when you believe it! The devil hates the Blood of Jesus, which defeated him at the Cross (Col. 2:15) and when Jesus was resurrected from the dead!

In the movie *The Passion of Christ*, there is a scene where Mary and another woman are whipping up the precious Blood of Jesus off the stone pavement with a cloth, not letting it be wasted, after He was beaten by the soldiers. There are books written about The Blood, but you can also look up Scriptures from the concordance at the back of your Bible, which is worth your time to develop your faith in its power!

Jesus took thirty-nine stripes for us. I have heard that doctors say that there are thirty-nine areas, or categories of the human body such as organs, bones, skin, brain, muscles, etc. that can have some kind of infirmity. So we can *claim those stripes, in exchange for our symptoms,* Jesus took and bore for us on the cross. Then do more than that, *take it by force*! Watch *The Passion of Christ* movie saying "**He did it for me!**"

Also, there are thirty-nine chapters in the Old Testament, could it be that when He said "It is finished!" (John 19:30) that it meant that His death on the cross, the 39 stripes, was the dividing line between the Old Testament (Law) and the New Testament (Covenant) sealed in His Blood, besides producing our redemption?

The Matzo bread that is eaten at Communion has the appearance of being pierced, bruised and scored as Jesus was beaten and whipped for us prior to His crucifixion. So *see your sicknesses, infirmities, dis-eases and pains* taken to hell and left there, where He shook them off and rose again healed! Believe He did it for you. So focus *on Jesus* with your symptoms nailed to the cross, and not on the symptoms! This means serious concentration, not a casual glance.

John 3:14,15: "And as Moses lifted up the serpent in the wilderness, even so must the Son of Man be lifted up: that whosoever believeth in Him should not perish, but have eternal life." This refers to Numbers 21:9: as the serpent on the pole (which was a type of Christ's crucifixion), caused all those that looked on it [AB: attentively, expectantly, with a steady and absorbing gaze] to live, after they were bitten by fiery serpents, when they complained and spoke against Moses. So once again, it wasn't a casual glance, or 'a drive through prayer' that healed them. They were desperate to get healed, *so they focused!*

For us that could mean studying the Word on all that the cross means to us, its implications and promises. Our healing, both spiritual and physical, comes from looking to and identifying with Christ crucified, by whose stripes you were healed. This is the Blood Covenant that we have, because of *Jesus obedience* to lay down His life for us. Hallelujah!! Thank you Jesus!

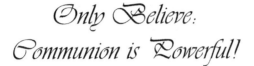

Chapter 10

Only Believe: Communion is Powerful!

Jesus said in Luke 22:20b: "This cup is the new testament in My blood, which is shed for you." _____ You need to put your name here and each time you take Communion. Mark 14:24 NKJV: "This is My blood of the new covenant,[35]which is shed for many."

"He that eateth My flesh, and drinketh My blood, dwelleth in Me, and I in him" (John 6:56). In John 6: 48, 51 Jesus says, "I am that bread of life. I am the living bread which came down from heaven: if any man eat of this bread, he shall live for ever: and the bread that I will give is my flesh, which I will give for the life of the world." In the Lord's Prayer, we say give us this day our daily bread, so you could say that we are asking *to receive Jesus for our day.* The way we do that is by spending time reading the Word, who is Jesus, letting Him reveal to us what He has to say each day.

When we take Communion, we eat some type of bread, cracker or Matzo as a symbol of eating His body, *believing* that it was broken *for our healing,* and is shed for many. (Matt.

---

[35] Strong's #1242 *covenant:* A will, testament, pact, contract, an agreed upon plan to which both parties subscribe. In the NT Jesus ratified by His death on the cross a new covenant, termed in Heb.7:22 "a better covenant."

26:28) He is our substitute carrying our diseases to the cross—
"in remembrance of me"—*His obedience and sacrifice of His own body for ours.*

The spotless Lamb of God: Because He had resisted temptation, never sinned, obeyed His father in all things, He had no disease in His body to get rid of, or sin in His life—spotless.

Also: "The cup of blessing which we bless, is it not the communion or sharing of the blood of Christ? The bread which we break, is it not the communion of the body of Christ?" (1 Cor. 10:16 NKJV) "Partakers of the covenant meal are also joined together in the body and blood of Christ. The blessings and responsibilities of the covenant are therefore extended laterally among those who partake of Christ together, as certainly as they are vertically between God and the believer in Christ."—Charles Simpson, see Contributors)

Referring to the Lord's Supper, 1 Corinthians 11:23–26 NKJV, the commentator says: ". . . is an opportunity to say, proclaim, or confess again: 'I herewith lay hold of all the benefits of Jesus Christ's full redemption for my life: forgiveness, wholeness, strength, health, and sufficiency.' The Lord's Supper is not to be simply a ritual remembrance, but an active confession, by which you actively will to call to memory and appropriate today all that Jesus has provided and promised through His Cross."—Roy E. Hayden, see Contributors

The blood is something wine-like (generally grape juice), taken in faith at Communion for forgiveness of sins (missing the mark), when you've received Him as Savior, giving you an opportunity to repent of anything you had done since your last Communion, which was not "pure, right, lovely or good report." He already knows about it, but requires us to humble ourselves and ask forgiveness. After that action, we have a clean slate, and *don't have anything the devil can condemn us for*, because he is the condemner, not God.

So after you have taken Communion, and accusations come to your mind, say: "**No, I am forgiven. That was taken care of at Communion on _____. I am the righteousness of God in Christ Jesus!**" and go on praising Him for His obedience to suffer for *you.*

So wouldn't we want to take Communion more seriously to settle the sin and healing issue in our lives? I do. I pray before I take Communion that the elements would be *anointed*, and that everyone taking it would receive what they are believing for, especially me.

The Divine Exchange: Ephesians 5:30: "For we are members of His body, of His flesh and of His bones." So doesn't this say Jesus wants us to have His healed, perfect body, instead of the symptoms on our bodies? He wouldn't bring the sickness, diseases and pains (which He bore on the cross for us and took into hell), with Him *when He abides in us.* That would not be loving or a benefit. That would keep us from doing the works of Jesus, sharing the Good News, casting out demons, healing the sick, and blessing others in many ways.

Remember in John 6:56 that Jesus said that if we eat His flesh and drink His blood we abide in Him—*He dwells in us.* And in 15:7 He said: "If ye abide in me, and my words abide in you, ye shall ask what ye will and it shall be done unto you." So when you spend quality time with the Lord, reading His word and are obedient to take Communion regularly, there is a reward. As you know, there is no one else who can give this promise for your prayer requests, which will be perfect for you. How loving is that!

Chapter 11

Only Believe:
The Word to Act!

If your faith is as small as a grain of mustard seed, you can still speak to your mountain, symptoms or problems to get rid of them. The footnote in the NKJV of Matthew 17:20 says, This mountain was a figure or an obstacle, hindrance, or humanly insurmountable problem—none of which is impossible for God to deal with through *committed people*, who accurately understand their authority, and know His power, will, purposes and provision. (Emphasis added)

Romans 10:17: "So then faith cometh by hearing and hearing by the word of God." If you don't read the Word, you won't find out all there is in it for you. Jesus said, "Therefore whosoever heareth these sayings of mine, and doeth them, I will liken him unto a wise man, which built his house upon a rock; and the rain descended, and the floods came, and the winds blew, and beat upon that house; and it fell not: for it was founded upon a rock" (Matt. 7:24, 25) So if you want to be wise, "Read the red and do what it says."

Everyone knows a rock is a solid foundation if it is on a flat surface, which is how firm we should be of our convictions, and trust in Jesus to help us in trouble. This only comes when you spend time with Him regularly, reading the Word about how he handled things while on earth, because He is the same yesterday, today and forever.

So read the New Testament *out loud*, and the Bible taught by anointed teachers. Get their CDs to listen to over and over again, which builds your faith on a particular topic. One man said he had been reading Revelation, and he wondered why he was having health problems. That's like going to California by turning east. Revelation has to do with the near future and nothing to do with ways to get healed. If you are doing something and it's not working, *change it*! He needed to meditate on what the Word says regarding health, and long life.

Hebrews 11: 1: "Now faith is . . ." God calls Himself the great I AM, Who is *now—in the present!* So believe NOW what Jesus has done for you in the past. He suffered greatly to give you health, soundness, peace and joy! Take it! He paid for it! Take the knowledge of it, receive it, and meditate on it!

"For this cause also thank we God without ceasing, because when ye received the Word of God which ye heard of us, ye received it not as the word of men, but as it is in truth, the word of God, which effectively worketh also in you that believe" (1 Thess. 2:13).

No word of God is without power to them that *believe*, which Paul speaks about in his prayer for us in Ephesians 1:19, 20a: "And what is the exceeding greatness of His power to us-ward who believe, according to the working of His mighty power, which He wrought in Christ".

It is written: "We are more than conquerors through him that loved us" (Rom. 8:37). So *we need to act like it*. Be persistent, insistent and shameless in your stand of faith for your healing, and restoration according to the Word. We have a covenant in the Blood of Jesus. He suffered and died to set us free and heal us!

Colossians 1:13,14: speaking of the Father, "Who hath delivered us from the power of darkness and hath translated us into the kingdom of his dear Son: in whom we have redemption through His blood, even the forgiveness of sins." *Past tense!* So get understanding of the Blood Covenant, so you can stand on it, which is a firm foundation for your healing.

Look to the cross as the Israelites were told to do to be healed of the snake bites in the desert, (the devil was first revealed as a snake in the Garden of Eden). Paul shook off the snake (viper) into the fire when it bit him, hidden in the sticks he picked up. (Acts 28:3–5) Don't allow yourself to be bitten by every sickness out there. Don't sign for the package of symptoms, when it knocks at your door. Say **"No thank you. Get off my property in Jesus' Name! I don't receive your lies!"** If you do have symptoms, shake them off into hell (the fire) like Paul did.

"He personally bore our sins in His [own] body on the tree [as on an altar and offered Himself on it] that we might die (cease to exist) to sin and live to righteousness. By His wounds you have been healed" (1Peter 2: 24 AB). This is looking *back at the cross* to Isaiah 53:4, 5. So look at Him. See Him doing this for you on the cross at Calvary, and not the symptoms!

Second Corinthians 4:18 says, "While we look not at the things which are seen, but at the things which are not seen [God's presence at your right hand, His faithfulness, His protection from harm, His promises of provision, His unfailing love, which are to be *believed by faith* in His word.] for the things which are seen are temporal, but the things which are not seen are eternal." *So symptoms are temporal or <u>subject to</u> <u>change</u>,* as we command them to bow the knee to the Name of Jesus—the Word of God!

We are to *resist the symptoms* by doing what Jesus did and *cast them out*, because they have no right to your body—*so deny their presence! Command* your body to line up with the Word that says you *were healed* through Jesus stripes! You are submitted to God and not the devil's lies! Paul said in 1 Corinthians 9:27 NKJV that he disciplined his body and brought it into subjection (submission). Notice he says *discipline his body*, which means he keeps it under control and doesn't let it do whatever it wants. It requires denial and self-control even if you have to speak to it, so use the Word that you have already learned and do it!

James 3:2b NKJV: "If anyone does not stumble in word, he is a perfect man, able also to bridle the whole body." So you could say**: "I command my body to line up and be in submission to the Word of God that says it's healed!"**

Charles Capps of *Charles Capps Ministries* said to slap that area of your body that is acting up, and speak the Word to it. Saying what the Word says activates the spiritual law of "sowing and reaping". By doing this over and over again, your body will learn to respond, and stop acting up. I've done this many times, and it works. Generally, it's just the enemy's lies.

Visualize Jesus suffering for you on the cross. Claim His substitution for you by faith, as if He were doing it right now! Say it like Mary did in Luke 1:38: "Be it unto me according to thy word." <u>Get serious</u>—the devil is. *Fight like a warrior!*

In Nahum 1:15, this is what God promised to do for Israel: "For the wicked shall no more pass through thee; he is utterly cut off."[36] For someone who has had Cancer, Pneumonia, Bronchitis, UTIs, Arthritis, or any other disease, you could say: "**The wicked one shall no more pass through me; he is utterly cut off in Jesus' Name!**" Then add: "**You will never hinder me again in Jesus' Name!**"

Joshua 17:13: "Yet it came to pass, when the children of Israel were waxen strong, that they put the Canaanites to tribute; but did not utterly drive them out." This wasn't the first time this Scripture is in the Old Testament; it shows up many times when the Israelites *did not totally wipe out* the nations God told them to.

It is the same way for us if we put up with symptoms, fears, unbelief or old mindsets when they first show up; they develop into *strongholds* in our bodies and lives. Then they become hard to get rid of and difficult to break (they have carved out a safe haven), just like demons have to have a body to live in to do their work in the world. (Matt. 8:28–32; Mark 5:1–4)

They will sway your way of thinking, as they linger in your body or mind. You can't let them weaken your faith just because you feel something. You have *to drive them out with the Word, the Name, the Blood* and *the faith of Jesus in you*—exercise your authority! You are more than a conqueror in Christ Jesus!

Then *cover yourself with the Blood,* until they have no place in you. Joshua spoke to Israel and said in 17:18c: "For thou shalt drive out the Canaanites [symptoms, fears, and old mind sets that go with them], though they have iron chariots, and though they be strong." He told them they had to do it themselves, sort of like a clearing a title to property. In 1 John 3:8 the Word

---

[36]   NKJV lit. one of Belial: one of the many names of satan meaning "worthlessness" or perhaps "lawlessness." (2 Cor. 6:15)

says, "For this purpose the Son of God was manifested, that he might destroy the works of the devil". Another translation says, "Came to the earth with the express purpose of liquidating the devil's activities."

Proverbs 14:19: "The evil bow before the good; and the wicked at the gates of the righteous." Because God loves you so much, He sent Jesus *to destroy, loosen, dissolve and liquidate* the devil's activities in your body and life. Believe it and claim it often. Believe the Word works!

The way you can act on this knowledge is to say every time you sneeze, cough, blow your nose, void, etc.: "**Thank You Jesus You are destroying, dissolving, liquidating and discarding the activities of the devil in my body now!**" Believe that you are being delivered! Then do what Jesus did, and thank God He heard you and always hears you. (John 11:41,42)

Next praise Him as if your deliverance was manifested in the natural, as the lame man did leaping and praising God exuberantly. (Acts 3) Act as though you have your healing now! Talk as if it is manifest in your life, and praise Him that it is accomplished. Don't focus on the symptoms, *only the Word*. Keep in mind the joy that is set before you like Jesus did, Who endured the cross, despised the shame for us. (Heb. 12:2) Continue to praise Him that you are healed until healing is manifested in your body.

Did you notice in 1 Peter 2:24 NKJV that by whose stripes [wounds] you were healed? If you hold your hand in front of your mouth, those words come back into you, instead of out into the air. So why not say to all your body parts: "**Head, trunk,**

abdomen, arms, legs, feet, etc. (from the top of your head to the souls of your feet) **with His stripes WE are healed!"**

Our bones, muscles, tendons, tissues, cells, organs, nails, arteries, veins, teeth, etc. are all included in our body. So *see them* being restored, whole and perfect. Post a picture of yourself when you were healthy, in a place you see often, to remind yourself what you should look like. Remember, God is a god of miracles, why not you?

I heard a pastor tell about a man that visualized armies of healthy white blood cells coming into his body and taking over the diseased cells (like Pac Man), because he believed that "all things are possible with God." (Matt. 19:26) He continued to do this often throughout his day, over and over again for weeks *until he was healed!* Just imagine how much better it will be if we speak like Jesus did, "It is written . . .," and the Scriptures over ourselves *regularly.* (Matt. 4:7)

In a partner letter I received, the minister wrote that we need to "become motor mouths and go full speed with the Word," without wavering, no matter how difficult it is, because that's faith. It is also how you conquer those mountains in your life and reach your goals. Most people aren't given raises, bonuses and rewards for doing nothing. They get them from working hard whether they feel like it or not.

In the story of the ten lepers that were healed when they cried out to Jesus for mercy, He told them *to do something*: "Go shew yourselves unto the priests. And it came to pass, that, as they went, they were cleansed" (Luke 17:13, 14). Their obedience to His command "go shew yourselves" brought them their healing, because *"they went."* You could say: **I am**

walking—"wenting" Lord, trusting in You to fulfill your Word to me as You cleansed the lepers, You cleanse me.

When King David and his army arrived home one day and found the city burned, and their families gone, they wept until they had no more power to weep. Then he asked God what to do. God said, "Pursue: for thou shalt surely overtake them, and without fail recover all" (1 Sam. 30:8). Verse 18 said that he recovered all. That would not have happened if *he had not done something*, probably saying as he pursued "God said I would overtake them and recover all. I believe God that it shall be as He has said." Good confession.

Now take Communion to establish it, with this point of contact. First Corinthians 11:24: "This do in remembrance of me." (Focus on Jesus triumph at the cross.) We are not to take His sacrifice lightly. Remember, God can't look at sin, and nothing can be hidden from His sight. So we need to *humbly examine ourselves* before Communion, and ask for forgiveness where ever we have *missed the mark*—sinned.

Make "a point of contact" (which is setting a thing, a location or time) when you Believed you received something *and you stick with it!* Step over an imaginary line on the floor, set the date, and stand praising God that you are healed! *Command your body* to function in the perfection which God created it to function, because it is written, with his stripes we are healed! Set your face like a flint on Jesus, (Isa. 50:7) and what He has done for you.

If you've seen any movie about the crucifixion, remind yourself of it by seeing it in your imagination, and that it is history! It is done! The Bible says He died once for all! (2 Cor. 5:15) You are one of the "all"!

Use the measure of faith God has given you
to receive your healing today,
and expect your breakthrough!

* * *

Faith as a Grain of Mustard Seed

Matthew 17:20 says:

> And Jesus said unto them, Because of your unbelief: for verily, I say unto you, If you have faith [that is living] as a grain of mustard seed, ye shall say unto this mountain, Remove hence to yonder place; and it shall remove; and nothing shall be impossible unto you.

A mountain is anything that hinders your progress, a problem, or a disease. Notice you are commanding it to move, by even the smallest amount of faith that you have by what you "say"! So even with a little faith, *you can make the situation change no matter how impossible it looks* according to this word. Now begin practicing this verse, as you follow the leading of the Holy Spirit one step at a time.

"As He was going into one village, He was met by ten lepers, who stood at a distance. And they raised up their voices and called, Jesus, Master, take pity *and* have mercy on us! And when He saw them, He said to them, Go [at once] and show yourselves to the priests. And so they went, they were cured *and* made clean. Then one of them, upon seeing that he was cured, turned back, recognizing and thanking and praising God with a loud voice; . . . And He said to him, Get up and go your way. Your faith (your trust and confidence that spring from your belief in God) has restored you to health" (Luke 17:12–19 AB)

The MSG: "One of them, when he realized he was healed, turned around and came back, shouting his gratitude, glorifying God. He kneeled at Jesus' feet so grateful. He couldn't thank Him enough—and he was a Samaritan . . . Jesus responded: Get up. On your way. Your faith has healed and saved you."

In obedience to the voice of Jesus, the nine ingrates were cleansed of leprosy, but the one who came back and worshiped Him was made well and restored to health. Remember lepers often had body parts destroyed from the disease, so this was a major blessing to this man for *worshiping Jesus*—the Healer—*and showing Him his gratitude.*

Just imagine what you can do if you *feed your faith with the Word* as a seed, it will grow, because: "Faith comes by hearing and hearing by the Word of God." So the more you feed your faith by reading the Word out loud, and listening to teachings about the Word, the more it will grow and become strong.

First John 4:17: "As he is, so are we in this world." So we are His hands and His feet to continue where He left off. He also said we would do greater things than He did. So our confessions should be in faith from your hearts, where we have sown the seeds. Then our *faith speaks in faith*, which pleases God to act!

The reason I've written about the importance of "saying", "believing" and "the Word" is because sometimes we need to hear it in *abundance* to break the old mindsets, bring revelation, and cause the breakthrough that we need.

Just like there are times we need an abundance of rain to stop the drought, to restore what appeared to be lost, and clean the streets, parking lots, and sidewalks, etc. That's why people go to seminars, conferences and buy books to get saturated in a particular topic, because we only 'believe half of what we hear and three quarters or what we see.'

The other reason is that no matter how many times I've shared the importance of reading the Word, believing it and saying what it says, I still keep hearing people's negative confessions, emotions and fears coming out of their mouths, which is easy to do. Unless you *diligently, consistently* put the Word first, *stay focused*, then *believe it* and *stand on it*, circumstances (plus the enemy), will steal your faith, blessings and joy.

> This book of the law shall not depart out of [thy mouth];
> but thou shalt [meditate therein day and night],
> that thou mayest observe [to do] according
> to all that is written therein:
> for then thou shalt make thy way prosperous,
> and then thou shalt have good success.
> — Joshua 1:8

God's Word Works

In Dr. Lilian B Yeomans book, His Healing Power,
she shares about creating a "faith home"
for terminally ill people.

One of these was a Christian woman
in the last stages of TB,
so Dr. Yeomans began treating her with God's medicine,
by reading her Scriptures on healing
from Genesis to Revelation.
She read over and over again Deuteronomy 28
and Galatians 3 regarding our redemption
from consumption, or TB.
Then she told her with every waking moment to say:
"According to Deuteronomy 28:22, consumption or
tuberculosis is a curse of the Law.
But according to Galatians 3:13,
Christ has redeemed me from the curse of the Law.
So Christ has redeemed me from tuberculosis."
The woman did this no matter how
weak she was for three days.
On the third day, Dr. Yeomans heard a commotion upstairs
that sounded like somebody had hit
the floor and was running.
Next she heard someone yelling,
"Dr. Yeomans" and rushing down the stairs,
hollering,"Dr, Yeomans! Did you
know I'm healed? I'm healed!
I'm the one who had the tuberculosis, but I'm healed!"

Harrison House 2003; www.harrisonhouse.com
(Used by permission)

* * *

We need to pray with faith and *belief* that *it is done—as if it already existed!* Praise as if you have received your answer in the natural! <u>Own it</u>! Praise healing is manifest on earth as it is in Heaven in your body now! Remember Mark 11:24 says, "What things soever ye desire, when ye pray, believe that ye receive them, and ye shall have them." "Signs will follow those who believe" (Mark 16:17).

So if you believe He has heard you, then praise Him that He is rewarding you with the answer to your faith confessions. If you have been diagnosed with some type of serious disease, visualize the doctor telling you that he can no longer find any evidence of the disease in your body. [I've read that this has happened to many people.] What would you do? Begin doing that NOW in faith!

Jesus Christ, the anointed Healer in me
worketh to deliver, heal and
restore my body now!

Chapter 12

Only Believe:
As Abraham Did

Romans 4:17, 18:

> (As it is written, I have made thee a father
> of many nations,) before him whom he believed,
> even God, who quickeneth the dead, and calleth
> those things which be not as though they were.
> Who against hope believed in hope, that he
> might become the father of many nations;
> according to that which was spoken, So shall
> thy seed be.[37]

Abraham—"And not being weak in faith[38], he did not
consider his own body, already dead (since he was about a
hundred years old), and the deadness of Sarah's womb He did
not waver at the promise of God through unbelief, but was

---

[37] NKJV verse: 18: Contrary to hope: Contrary to ordinary human
expectation. In hope: in expectation that God would fulfill His
promises.

[38] *Faith:* Mark 11:22 Strong's #4102 NKJV says: it means conviction,
confidence, trust, belief, reliance, trustworthiness, and persuasion. It
is the divinely implanted principle of inward confidence, assurance,
trust, and reliance in God and all that He says. The word sometimes
denotes the object or content of *belief.*

strengthened in faith, giving glory to God and being fully convinced that what He had promised He was also able to perform (Rom. 4:19–21 NKJV).

He *ignored* the conditions he could see, and feel about himself and Sarah's history of bareness, *trusting God's word only.* He made a decision (a choice) to believe God's promise! He said to himself "I don't care what the circumstances look like. I believe God and that settles it!" That's why he's called the Father of Faith.

Second Corinthians 5:7: "For we walk by faith, not by sight." Or you might say, **"We believe even if we can't see it or feel it!"** That's faith! Remember Jesus said: "Blessed are they that have not seen, and yet have believed."

These Roman Scriptures always encourage me and jerk up my slack! Just think about his circumstance, and how he had to stand trusting God for years, when he heard so little from Him, even thou it was in a mighty way. He didn't have a Bible to encourage him everyday like we do, that says in Mark 10:27: "With men it is impossible, but not with God; for with God all things are possible."

He had to keep telling himself: "*God* told me I would be the father of many nations, so He knows how that is going to happen to a very old man with a barren wife." Notice he did not waver at the promise of God through unbelief, for the fulfillment of a seemingly impossible promise, but he was *strengthened* (encouraged) *when he gave God glory*—praised Him. He is our example.

> Even as Abraham believed God, and it was accounted to him for righteousness. Know ye therefore that they which are of faith, the same

are the children of Abraham . . . But that no man is justified by the law in the sight of God, it is evident: for, The just shall live by faith. And the law is not of faith: but the man that doeth them shall live in them. Christ hath redeemed us from the curse of the law, being made a curse for us: for it is written, Cursed is every one that hangeth on a tree: that the blessing of Abraham might come on the Gentiles through Jesus Christ; that we might receive the promise of the spirit through faith (Gal. 3:6,7,11–14).

The curse of the law is Deuteronomy 28:15–68, but verse 61 says, "Also every sickness and every plague, which is not written in the Book of the Law." So even if your symptoms are not listed in the curse verses, it is covered in this verse as being the ones Jesus bore for you on the cross, which means you are redeemed[39] from them!

The Bible never says that Abraham had any kind of sickness, so I take that blessing of health and long life also!

The blessing of Abraham: "I will make of thee a great nation, I will bless[40] thee and make thy name great; and thou shalt be a blessing: and I will bless them that bless thee, and curse him who curseth thee; and in thee shall all the families of the earth be blessed". This is the verse that is referred to regarding

---

[39]   *Redeem* means (v) to buy back, or clear, to restore; to free from the consequence of sin. Merriam-*Webster Inc*

[40]   NKJV Luke 6:28, Strong's #2127 - *bless:* to speak well of . . . *bless abundantly.* When God blesses men, He grants them *favor* and confers happiness upon them.

the concept of "The Blessing": God at work in the lives of His people to counter the effects of "the curse". (Gen. 12:2, 3 NKJV)

So if you see your symptoms in the curse in Deuteronomy 28:15–68, say "**Since_____ is a curse, and I believe Jesus became a curse for me according to Galatians 3:13, paid the price for it, took it, I no longer have it! Thank you Jesus! I'm redeemed from that curse for You became a curse for me. Hallelujah!**" Now write down the date, and continue to praise him for your redemption, as if you have it manifested now, because you *believe* you have it by faith!

Romans 4:17 is the verse that the "Name it claim it" Christians base their confession on. "Before him whom he believed, even God, who quickeneth the dead, and calleth those things which be not as though they were." God is our example, and He did it here when He called those things: "Abraham the father of many nations", that was not yet as though it were—that's faith! (Also Mark 11:23, 24) So calling yourself redeemed from the curse, is your faith talking—Scriptural.

Wise Disciplines for a Believer: (Behaving like a Christian)

When you first get up, *anoint yourself with oil* according to Ecclesiastes 9:8 NKJV, "And let your head lack no oil." The oil is a type or symbol of the Holy Spirit in the Bible, and a point of contact. My experience with "anoint" as I was taught *is Christ on me* to do what I could not normally do. It is doing with ease whatever I need to do, so I pray this for others when they need to deal with or accomplish something.

So put a small amount of olive oil in a vial of some type (an empty cologne or after shave bottle), taking a drop onto your finger and lift it up to the Lord; then ask Him to "anoint it with the Holy Spirit and mix it with the Blood of Jesus", *believing* He heard you.

Then touch the top of your head saying: "I anoint myself and . . . (name anyone else, because there is no distance with Spirit) in the Name of Jesus." Now touch your forehead asking God to take control of your conscious, subconscious, an unconscious mind, words, thoughts and actions.

Next touch your eyes and ask that your spiritual eyes be opened and see, (fingers on ears) your spiritual ears be opened and hear, (hand on the center of your body where your Spirit is) and that you would receive whatever God wants you to know that day. (Matt. 13:15) Don't you want to know every thing the Lord wants you to know for your day, and for Him to take care of your loved ones?

Last, I ask that my work (thumbs and big toes) and my walk would be anointed. (Ex. 29:20) See Lev. 8:5, 10–12, 23, 30; 9:23

We are ambassadors for Christ
—2 Corinthians 5:20a

Be a doer of the Word and not a hearer only. (James 1:22) Follow the leading of the Holy Spirit, and do the things He puts on your heart to do, *even if you have to do it in faith.* (Putting it off is disobedience.) As you follow His leading, more will be revealed to you and you will be amazed at how easy it was to do.

He has all your days written in His book, so ask Him what He wants you to do (to be in agreement with His plan for you), and you will prosper and be safe. Remember that God is love, and He will do the best thing for your life when you are obedient to him, and sometimes when you're not because of His abundant mercy. I prefer a sure thing—obedience!

Walk in love *even if you have to do it in faith*, treating others as you would have them treat you—the Golden Rule. "Let all that you do be done with love" (1 Cor. 16:14 NKJV). If you don't know how to "Walk in love'", get a book on it like *Limitless Love* through *Kenneth Copeland Ministries*, which is a daily devotional. We need to be reminded daily, because we are always tempted to walk in selfishness—the flesh.

Be a person of excellence, remembering that you may be the only Christian that the people around you may know. So be faithful, diligent, honest, and generous. Look for people to bless. Observe and listen when you are around them for some way to bless them. Think of others more highly than yourself. Say to yourself "What would Jesus do?" Then do it!

Ladies, how you dress will cause you to be respected or not—asking for trouble. So don't wear anything that you could not *wear in front of Jesus* and feel comfortable. Remember you are an ambassador for Him, and an example of how a Christian should act and dress.

> Present your bodies a living sacrifice,
> holy, acceptable unto God,
> which is your reasonable service.
> —Romans 12:1

Eat a healthy diet of five to nine fresh fruits and vegetables each day, especially berries and asparagus, which are antioxidants and kidney detoxifiers. Drink half your weight in ounces of water every day and take probiotics regularly, which will protect you from many viruses, etc.

Fast occasionally, as the Lord leads to spend more time with Him, praying, reading the Word, and before Communion. Ezra 8:23 NKJV: "So we fasted and entreated our God for this, and He answered our prayer." (of protection)

You can 'fast' many ways, just ask Him what you should give up. *Don't listen to your flesh* that says you don't need to exercise, drink water, you need more dessert or a snack. Fasting is good for the soul, and you'll be glad you did it, when you *spend your time wisely.* Remember the apostle Paul said I beat my body into subjection. As athletes train their bodies to win, *train your body to obey you* and not the other way around.

> Put a knife to your throat,
> if you are a man given to appetite.
> —Proverbs 23:2 NKJV

Remember, you are now "the temple of the Holy Spirit" (1 Cor. 3:16), so *feed Him the Word* to cause Him to flourish in you. A carnal Christian is one who has made their flesh and their belly their god. (Phil. 3:19) The Word warns about this: "For to be carnally minded is death; but to be spiritually minded is life and peace" (Rom. 8:6).

So if you can't control your appetite, why would you think demons would listen to you when you try to cast them out, if you are walking in such fear that you are not going to get enough to eat? Jesus said to His disciples when they couldn't cast out demons, these only come out with prayer and fasting.

(Matt. 17:21) It requires discipline. Be careful of the lust of the flesh. You don't need everything you see.

> But put ye on the Lord Jesus Christ,
> and make not provision for the flesh,
> to fulfil the lusts thereof.
> —Romans 13:14

The Holy Spirit is your Comforter, not more and more food, which causes Diabetes, obesity, Cancer, inflammation, etc. etc. Whatever you sow you reap, so sow to the Spirit and reap blessings. (Gal. 6:7, 8) Sow to the flesh and reap destruction: misery, surgeries, drugs, the loss of your money, lost time doing what you want to do or need to do, etc.

Get fresh air and exercise regularly. Pray and praise while you are exercising; don't just let your mind be idle. Prepare an MP3 player with your faith confessions, and plug them into your ears, so you can confess them while you exercise. You'll be encouraged when you do. Why just listen to music or whatever? We are to think on things that are pure, right, lovely and of good report (Phil. 4:8), which is a perfect description of Jesus. Then speak those things.

A merry heart doeth good like a medicine (Prov.17:22). The Knox version says: "A cheerful heart makes a quick recovery." So watch movies and television programs that are entertaining and uplifting—anything that you could watch with Jesus in the room. In everything you have a choice what you watch or listen to. Choose wisely and ask yourself: What benefit do I receive from watching or listening to this? Psalms 119:37 NKJV says, "Turn away my eyes from looking at worthless things, and revive me in Your way." Yes!

Pay tithes (Lev. 27:30; Mal. 3:10) of the first ten percent of your gross income where the Lord leads each week. The Word talks about giving to that ministry where you have benefited. (1 Cor. 9: 11–14) I am amazed week after week when I see an empty offering plate passed to me, that people have come "empty handed" (Deut.16:16 NKJV) especially when all our needs are met in a clean comfortable church, and salaries need to be paid to those that minister the Gospel through the Word, or music. How much work do you do each week without being paid? How much more should we do for the people of God that serve us?

Then **Name your** "seed" sown to the Lord's work, expecting to receive a return according to the "law of sowing and reaping". (Gal. 6:7) *You can't receive a harvest if you don't plant seed!* You might say: "I'm cheerfully sowing this seed that God's Word would be manifested in my life as He has promised." Jesus said: "Give, and it shall be given unto you; good measure, pressed down, and shaken together, and running over, shall men give into your bosom. For with the same measure that ye mete withal it shall be measured to you again" (Luke 6:38).

So everyone that does not give their tithe, or offering are missing out on this promise, and are actually in disobedience to His Word, besides the blessing of increase that goes with it. Actually we are to give tithes *and* offerings, not just your leftovers. I wonder what these people will tell the Lord when they are in great need, because they have not placed anything in 'the banks of Heaven', and trusted His faithfulness to perform His Word.

Get agreement with your spouse and family members for added strength in your prayers, and to bring forth the answer you need in whatever you are praying for. (Matt. 18:19) See details in *Spiritual Warfare* : Chapter 13

Pray for others to be healed. Make a list of the people that you know that need healing, and *pray for them daily as you do for yourself*, expecting to be healed also, according to James 5:16 "Pray one for another, that ye may be healed."

Don't get offended at anything someone says about you, or doesn't do for you. We need to *forgive others*, including family members, as Christ has forgiven us, so our prayers will not be hindered. (1 Peter 3:7) Then cast that care upon the Lord, leaving it in His hands, (1 Peter 5:7) and *don't think about it!* When the thought comes back (it's probably the devil or your flesh), cast it down! Sometimes you may have to do this procedure over and over again in order to get your victory or peace about it. I've found praying in the spirit works the best focusing on Jesus.

Replace it with "That's not my thought. It's in the Lord's Hands", and *purposely* think of something true, noble, just, pure, and of good report . . . anything praise worthy—Jesus! Then pray for their needs to be met, also. Read Hebrews 13:1–17, and the prayer in 20 and 21.

Be aware that the devil will try to *discourage you anyway he can.* That's why reading the Bible daily can strengthen you, and *encourage* you while you wait for your prayers to be answered. If you follow the leading of the Holy Spirit, many times you will pick up a book, devotional, or watch a ministry that is teaching just what you need to hear. Remember you are not the only one that gets discouraged. Often a minister will share what he or she has been dealing with and how they overcame it.

Anytime I'm discouraged I pray in the Spirit, read one of my favorite books that had encouraged me before, and praise the Lord; even doubling up on my faith confessions or listening to a CD in one of the locations I'm in for awhile. Then the Counselor generally gives me just what I need. I don't run from God, but to God—my Source for everything. He already knows what's going on and *how to get me through it,* if I'll just follow the leading of the Holy Spirit.

Memorize Scripture: We should know the healing Scriptures so well that no one, no demon *or feeling can talk us out of them!* [Pain doesn't change God's Word!] God wants us to *believe Him* in the face of everything that is contrary to His Word. You need to have such *faith* that you can do the works of Jesus.

When a storm, high winds or a tornado is forecasted, *speak to it as Jesus did*: **Peace!** Then commission angels to break it up, dissipate it, and tell it not to come near your home, because it is written: no weapon formed against you shall prosper . . . no plague or calamity come near your dwelling in Jesus' Name. (Isa. 54:17; Ps. 91:10) *Plead the Blood of Jesus over* your home, trees, neighborhood, power coming to your home, etc. I have done this many times, and sometimes gotten out of bed to do the commanding when a storm came unexpectedly during the night. We've never had damage, and rarely a power outage when it is in our area. Praise the Lord!

So be prepared by keeping the Word, and the promises God has given you ever before you. Double up on the Word and your faith confessions when it seems to be taking a long time, as you stand praising God, because you believe you RECEIVED YOUR ANSWER!

> In all these things
> we are more than conquerors.
> —Romans 8:37

Read good devotionals like *365 Days of Healing* by Mark Brazee, *World Outreach Church*, who teaches from the Bible on various aspects of healing, with faith confessions; and also *God Calling* (*Barbour*), which is a daily devotional written by two listeners about what Jesus said to them each day. [It has blessed and encouraged me for years, and I've given many copies away.]

See the Recommended Books at the end also. *Christ the Healer*, is an excellent book, which contains the sermons and teachings of F.F. Bosworth, who God used mightily in the years of his ministry. The book shares testimonies of miracles of healings, when everything else had been done by the medical field (without any results), and are amazing! Generally after hearing him teach, *people were anointed, prayed for <u>and healed</u>!* which caused them and the people that knew them to be "saved" *and* sometimes healed also.

Most often, because of their gratitude, they told others and even went to teach and heal the sick. Their joy produced a life of service to God as His servants. Matthew 8:14, 15 tells about Jesus healing Peter's mother-in-law, and she arose and ministered to them. Our motive should be to be healed, so we can do the work God called us to do with all our strength. We can't help anyone if we're weak or in pain.

*Praise Him continually
for your healing.*

Chapter 13

Only Believe: You Have Authority!

"So Abraham prayed unto God: and God healed Abimelech, his wife, and his maid servants: and they bare children" (Gen. 20:17).

"And the Lord hearkened to Hezekiah, and healed the people" (2 Chron. 30:20).

"The earnest (heartfelt, continued) prayer of a righteous man makes tremendous power available (dynamic in its working)" (James 5:16b AB). So if we want to see change in our circumstances we must pray *earnestly, fervently and with energy*—"The effective, fervent prayer of a righteous man avails much." NKJV

"Bless the Lord, ye His angels, that excel in strength, that do His commandments, hearkening unto the voice of His word" (Ps.103:20). "Are they not all ministering spirits, sent forth to minister for them who shall be heirs of salvation?" (Heb.1:14 NKJV) So we need to be sure the words we are speaking are the Word, if we want angels to help us (saints), because that is what they do. If you are not speaking the Word, they can't help you.

Because Daniel was a praying man (10:10–13), an angel came to him and said, "Daniel: for from the first day that thou didst set thine heart to understand, and to chasten thyself before thy God, thy words were heard; and I am come for thy words." Notice the angel said "from the first day" he decided to get God's thoughts and humble himself, *his words*, not his thoughts, *were heard*, and the angel came in response to give him understanding regarding the vision. So man can have encounters with angels for a purpose.

"You shall also decide and decree[41]a thing, and it shall be established for you; and the light [of God's favor] shall shine upon your ways" (Job 22:28 AB). Since Jesus said to say: To speak aloud; to express oneself in words. So if we want something to change in our life, we can't just think it, wish it, hope it, we must SAY, speak out loud, *decree, declare*, proclaim, profess, announce, make full claim to, *prophesy*, and say emphatically what we want to happen! Say it like Jesus would say it, because you now *live by the faith of the Jesus.* (Rev. 14:12) Exercise your authority over the circumstance, or your body.

Jesus exercised His authority when he went to the temple and "began to cast out them that sold and bought in the temple, and overthrew the tables of the moneychangers, and the seats of them that sold doves; and would not suffer that any man should carry any vessel through the temple" (Mark 11:15,16). This is after He cursed the fig tree, and it is called *righteous anger*, because what they were doing was not right! So if something is not right, or agrees with the Word, follow the leading of the Holy Spirit to make it right!

Ezekiel 37:1–10 is called "Resurrection of dry bones" where the Lord's Hand was upon him, and told him to "Prophesy upon these bones, and say unto them, O ye dry bones, hear the word

---

[41] *Decree*: an official order given by a person with power. *Merriam-Webster Inc*

of the Lord." Then He told him to speak breath into them, and sinews and flesh, etc. *and it happened,* as he obeyed the Lord while the Spirit was *upon* him. The Old Testament term was "the hand of the Lord" was upon a person. (Ezra 8:18) After Pentecost, it is the anointing of the Holy Spirit *inside a person* that leads them regarding what to do. See *Only Believe*: the Holy Spirit, chapter 3.

God was showing him how He saw Israel and what he wanted Ezekiel to do about it as His servant. So even what looks dead and hopeless can be raised up to new life, when we are anointed *to prophesy*[42] or speak as if divinely inspired *to it.* All things are possible to him that believes, so obey Him!

This might be a case of Emphysema, Arthritis, or a dry marriage. Start speaking to it as God spoke to the darkness— the void: "And God said, Let there be light: and there was light (Gen. 1:3). Do it with the God kind of faith that believes!

Exercise Your Power and Authority!

"And when He had called unto him his twelve disciples, he gave them power against unclean spirits, to cast them out, and to heal all manner of sickness and all manner of disease." (Matt.10:1) So it's the will of God, and the *love of God* for you to be delivered and healed.

Matthew 11:12 AB: "And from the days of John the Baptist until the present time, the kingdom of heaven has endured violent assault, and violent men seize it by force [as a precious prize—a share in the heavenly kingdom is sought with most ardent zeal and intense exertion]."

---

[42]   *Merriam-Webster Inc*

NKJV footnote says: "The violent then [who take it by force] are people of keen enthusiasm and commitment, who are willing to respond to and propagate with radical abandonment the message and dynamic of God's reign." [Don't be like Pharaoh, who told Moses to get rid of the frogs tomorrow. (Ex.8; 8–10) Do you want to deal with the symptoms another day or night?]

If you want your miracle, you have to <u>press in</u>, and *press through when you don't feel like it*, and <u>take it by force</u>! when you believe God is leading you to take the next step. Sometimes if you don't, you will be robbed, because you've missed your opportunity, and may even lose your authority against the enemy. He knows if you mean business.

Believe that the Holy Spirit will do the work when you make a command. He is the Implementer. That is why it is so important *to know your Father's voice,* which only comes by spending time with Him in close fellowship.

"And I will give unto thee the keys of the kingdom of heaven: and whatsoever thou shalt bind [forbid] on earth will be bound [forbidden] in heaven: and whatsoever thou shalt loose on earth shall be loosed in heaven" (Matt.16:19).

If Jesus gave us "the keys of the kingdom of Heaven", then He must have thought *we needed them* to live like Heaven on earth. He didn't expect us to stick them in a drawer and forget about them. He knew He was only going to be on earth for a little while longer, so He had to teach and prepare His followers for all they would be dealing with when He left.

[I hope this book gets into the hands of people with PTSD, because it is your answer to this destructive condition. There is nothing that can help you as fast as reading, receiving and implementing the truths that I have listed in *Only Believe!*, except if you get counseled and prayed for by a Spirit-filled Believer that will exercise their authority, and deliver you from that demonic oppression. Then you must read and confess the Word daily until all symptoms are gone. Also you must renew your mind to who you are in Christ Jesus, and more than a conqueror! After that go out and help others, since you know what they are dealing with.]

With all that is going on around the world right now, we need to be doing what Jesus taught us to do to protect ourselves, our families, our possessions, our churches, friends, our military and our country—this life as we know it.

Every day the News or Weather Channel reports of disasters, killings, kidnappings, corruption, and strange happenings somewhere around the world or in your neighborhood. There are no longer reports of one or two tornadoes, but 15-30 sometimes in a day or night! There are records being broken frequently re: temperatures, depths of snow or rain, new signs and weather conditions we've never seen or heard before—signs of the end times, which Jesus spoke about. (Matt. 24)

Remember the enemy comes to kill, steal and destroy, and *he will use any one or situation to do it.* You have not if you ask not. (James 4:2) So ask God to back you up, when you *pray in faith*, exercising your authority according to His perfect will, which is His Word.

Greater is He that is in [you],
than he that is in the world.
—1 John 4:4b

I do this every day, and sometimes more than once in prayer for my day, family, our church, friends, our military, missionaries, our government, this country, Israel and the world. This is in obedience to 1 Tim. 2:1–4 which says, "I exhort therefore, that, first of all, supplications, prayers, intercessions and giving of thanks, be made for all men; for kings, and for all that are in authority; that we may lead a *quiet and peaceable life in all godliness and honesty. For this is good and acceptable in the sight of God our Saviour; who will have *all men to be saved, and to come unto the knowledge of the truth.*" (Emphasis added) [*So God doesn't think loud boisterous behavior that takes someone else's peace is right; or that lying and taking advantage of a situation is right either— it's ungodly!]

I feel a strong responsibility to pray the weekly prayer requests from *The Presidential Prayer Team* website (G W Bush started it in 2001), and I do it no matter where I am daily, even at those times when we had to get up at 2:30 in the morning for an early flight. I believe my prayers have protected our relatives no matter where they live. If you were around me when I pray, you would clearly hear that I am a bold, fervent prayer warrior to stop the enemy in every way I can, and protect God's servants and children where ever they are with the Word.

Besides that, I pray about the weather forecasted, and circumstances that come up during the day that I don't believe agree with Heaven. I exercise my authority believing God hears me as I remind Him of His Word; then I "cast the care" of it upon Him to bring it to pass according to His will. We do all we can do and then stand praising God.

When Jesus was awakened from sleep by his disciples during "a great tempest" on the sea, which almost sank their boat, He *rebuked* the wind and the sea, saying "Peace, be still! And the wind ceased and there was a great calm" (Mark 4:39). Since *rebuke* means to reprehend sharply; to reprimand, to *reprove*, it makes sense to say Jesus commanded[43] the weather conditions to rage no more. He stopped them!

So if Jesus taught by example, and we see severe weather conditions coming, shouldn't we exercise our authority and stop it from destroying life and property? Yes, of course! That is why we need to read the Bible to see how He handled all the various harmful circumstances, and do what He did. "Read the red and do what it says!" Do it with the same *faith of Jesus* Who had faith in His father to back him up. Remember, "Christ in you, the hope of glory" (Col. 1:27c).

So once again, when you see or hear of a destructive weather forecast for your area, begin speaking to it to cease and desist! Rebuke it, command the thing: damaging winds, hail, torrential rains, etc. to stop, say: "That's enough!" Commission angels to break it up, dissipate it, which causes it to lose its power to destroy. Do what Jesus did *in faith* to the winds and the waves and say "Peace, be still!" Stand your ground and protect your home and property with your words of faith. Follow the leading of the Holy Spirit regarding the conditions, whether you command it to be taken up into the storehouses, or whatever—*obey.*

---

43   In Matt. 8:26 NKJV, which is the same situation, the footnote states that this demonstrates Jesus' authoritative reign over the entire Earth, including inclement elements that might find their source in the destructive power of the 'evil one'.

Then claim *the Blood of Jesus* over your home, lives, property, power coming to our house and neighborhood. Say: **"It is written: "No weapon formed against me shall prosper!" No plague or calamity come near my dwelling in Jesus' Name!** Get somebody to agree with you, also. Don't allow the enemy to kill, steal and destroy. *Enforce* the protection with the Word you've learned, and then praise God for the Word, the Blood, the wisdom and authority He has given you.

Do this also for problems, symptoms or any other trouble, and command them to be removed and planted into the sea (Luke 17:6); and forbid them to come back in Jesus' Name! (Mark 9:25) *Don't back down;* keep speaking words of faith over the situation like peace, health, prosperity, favor, harmony, restoration and joy—what you want or desire.

Jesus said, "And these signs will follow them that believe: In My name shall they cast out devils; . . . they shall lay hands on the sick and they shall recover" (Mark 16:17, 18d, 20). That sounds like *taking the situation by force to improve it,* deliver and heal. In these verses, He tells His disciples what will happen when they do what He told them to do as they *believe:* cast out devils, speak with new tongues; and lay hands on the sick, and they shall recover; *and* He will work with them and confirm the word with signs following.

All these Scriptures, spoken by Jesus after He gave His disciples power and authority are for Believers also. God has given us instructions how to live on this earth, and how to *handle the enemy with boldness,* because *we believe the Word and act on it.* Just as Jesus said that He does what He sees His father doing, we need to do what we see Jesus doing in the Word. He is the way, the truth and the life—our example.

That's why God sent Him: *a living instruction book* to better life.

We need to stop thinking we have to wait until something happens, because He has given us His Holy Spirit, His Word, the keys to the kingdom, authority, the mind of Christ, angels that hearken to the Word when we speak it (Ps.103:20), and the anointing to do it when He leads us. It is written: "Because as he is, so are we in this world" (1 John 4:17b). So ask yourself, "What would Jesus do?" and do it! Jesus healed by His word, His touch, the virtue in Him, His compassion or according to the need. See examples below:

Matt. 8:16: "When the even was come, they brought unto him many that were possessed with devils: and he cast out the spirits with his word, and healed all that were sick"

Luke 18:15:"And they brought unto him also infants, that he would touch them"

Luke 6:19: "And the whole multitude sought to touch him: for there went virtue out of him, and healed them all."

Matt. 14:14: "And Jesus went forth, and saw a great multitude, and was moved with compassion toward them, and he healed their sick."

Matt. 9:35: "And Jesus went about all the cities and villages, teaching in their synagogues, and preaching the gospel of the kingdom, and healing every sickness and every disease among the people."

Jesus Christ is the same yesterday, today and forever.
—Hebrews 13:8

Spiritual Warfare

When Jesus gave his disciples *power[44] and authority over all demons, and to cure diseases*, it was similar to when the Lord took the Spirit that was on Moses and put it on the seventy elders in Numbers 11:17—*a divine transfer of the Spirit*, which He also did when God took our sins and sicknesses and placed them on Jesus at the cross. (Luke 9:1; Mark 3:15) Powerless ministries become powerful upon discovering the *exousia* power resident in the Name of Jesus and the Blood of Jesus! (Mark 3:16 NKJV notes)

To grasp the power of the *Name of Jesus and His blood*, look up Scriptures, or get specific teaching on them like *The Word, The Name, The Blood* by Joyce Meyer. Study and *believe* in these two powerful tools for your prayer life; they will save you, as they have saved others, when you *believe* in them.

Luke 10:19: "Behold, I give unto you power to tread on serpents and scorpions, and over all the power of the enemy: and nothing shall by any means hurt you." Notice Jesus promised "nothing shall be any means hurt you" to give you confidence, instead of fear. When I do spiritual warfare every morning, I say after binding the principalities and powers and rulers of the darkness of this world in Jesus' Name, and "nothing shall by any means will hurt me!" which *shuts the door to the enemy immediately*, because I have faith in this promise. (Eph. 6:12)

---

[44] Power–*exousia*: Mk 3:16 NKJV, Strong's #1849 means the authority or right to act, ability, . . . capacity, *delegated authority*. Jesus gave His followers *exousia* to preach, teach, heal, and deliver, and that authority has never been rescinded.

With all the terrorist groups that are killing and destroying people's lives, homes, churches, etc. in the News daily, shouldn't we be doing our part by exercising the authority Jesus gave us—Believers—to stop their activities in our area, and nation? That's why Paul taught that "We wrestle not against flesh and blood, but against principalities, against powers, against the rulers of the darkness of this world, against spiritual wickedness in high places" (Eph.6:12).

So terrorists are ruled by demonic spirits: principalities, powers, rulers of the darkness (satan) and spiritual wickedness in high places, because they have allowed them into their minds and lives by what they have been taught by their leaders *and* obeyed.

Could it be why Jesus taught by example, gave us His Name and the promise that if we believed when we prayed, He would answer? Yes, He already said there would be wolves that would come in after His departure (Acts 2:29), and shared about all the end time events in Matthew 24, that we are seeing happening in the world today. Then He tells us "Be sober, be vigilant; because your adversary the devil, as a roaring lion, walketh about, seeking whom he may devour: who resist[45] stedfast in the faith, knowing that the same afflictions are accomplished in your brethren that are in the world"[46] (1 Peter 5: 8, 9). If we don't pray, resist and withstand these evil powers, who will?

---

[45] The footnote in the NKJV: *Resist*: an assertive stance against the Adversary's operations. Christians must be spiritually alert, not only to withstand his attacks, but in prayer and spiritual warfare opposing him.

[46] Eph. 6:13 *Strong's #436 NKJV: suggests vigorously opposing, bravely resisting, standing face-to-face against an adversary, standing your ground... with the authority and spiritual weapons granted to us, we can withstand evil forces.

> Because sentence against an evil work
> is not executed speedily,
> therefore the heart of the sons of men
> is fully set in them to do evil.
> —Ecclesiastes 8:11

I've told this so many times: when Hitler was beginning his annihilation of the Jews, He went to the church in Germany and talked to them. They didn't do anything! So he was not controlled in his activities as history records. The people gave him an inch and he took the whole country, and destroyed thousands of lives.

Don't be too busy or complacent to stop the enemy in his tracks with your authority in Jesus' Name. People always think someone else is going to do it. Corporate prayer is powerful! Decide to be a "prayer warrior" in the kingdom of God!

So as a lion tamer holds up a chair in front of the roaring lion to distract him, your daily *prayers of faith*, your *exercise of authority* in the Word, will protect you and your loved ones when you *believe*, from his attacks.

Since the devil comes to kill, steal and destroy, if we don't take authority over him and kick him out of our lives daily, he'll give you trouble, because he is "the troubler". When Jesus was in the wilderness being troubled by him, the devil left after hearing "It is written", several times, "until an opportune time." (Luke 4: 4,13) So the devil can't argue with the Word when it is *spoken in faith*, not just thought. Don't let him catch you unaware!

The more you know and believe the Word, the more ammunition you have against him. Jesus said in John 8:31b, "If ye continue in My word, then are ye My disciples indeed; And ye shall know the truth, and the truth shall make you free." Wouldn't knowing the truth of what belongs to you through Jesus, make you free from the lies of the devil? Yes, of course it would. So *receive your freedom* by reading the Truth daily.

If Jesus had attacks from the enemy throughout His ministry, why do we think the enemy won't bother us with his lies, and symptoms? James 4:7 says, "Submit yourselves therefore to God. Resist the devil, and he will flee from you." *Resist the symptoms or lies* that don't agree with the truth that says: "By Whose stripes you were healed". *There may be days you will have to do this over and over again,* as you speak your faith confessions, because *he is trying to get you to stop believing the Word is true. Don't give in!*

Second Corinthians 10:3–5 (Amplified):

> For though we walk (live) in the flesh, we are not carrying on our warfare according to the flesh and using mere human weapons. For the weapons of our warfare are not physical [weapons of flesh and blood], but they are mighty before God for the overthrow and destruction of strongholds, [inasmuch as we] refute arguments and theories and reasonings and every proud and lofty thing that sets itself up against the [true] knowledge of God; and we lead every thought and purpose away captive into the obedience of Christ (the Messiah, the Anointed One)

Please take this seriously! God wouldn't have put it in His Word to "Put on the whole armor of God, that you may be able to stand against the wiles/schemings of the devil" *if we didn't need it!* (Eph. 6:11 NKJV) Verse 13 says, "Therefore take up the whole armor of God, that you may be able to withstand in the evil day, and having done all, to stand."

Notice it says "in the evil day", that day is *when circumstances are challenging your faith in God's Word.* This is when you confess it more, because you *believe* that God's Word is final authority in your life. The Word does not return void (Is. 55:11), it is living and powerful, which says *circumstances are subject to change,* because *they can be lies of the devil,* who comes to steal, kill and destroy your peace and anything else he can.

Remember, he comes to steal the Word (sometimes immediately by distractions), you have sown in your heart, because he knows it is the power which causes *you to stand* and not give up, even if it looks like nothing is working on your behalf. That's why it says "having done all, to stand." So your ability to *stand* comes from the Word, when you sow it into your heart.

When you make the decision to make God's Word final authority, you are *believing Jesus will be faithful* to the promises He has given you, and will back them up. He is able! Just like what happened to the Believers that went forth and preached everywhere, "the Lord working with them, and confirming the Word with signs following" (Mark 16:20). You are a Believer also, *so expect Him to back you up!*

In Ephesians 6:18 after putting on the whole armor of God, the Word says, "Praying always with all prayer and supplication in the Spirit, and watching thereunto with all perseverance and supplication for all saints;" So to help you *stand*, enlist the Holy Spirit's prayer language, *which will be the perfect will of God*. Without it you can only pray what you know. You are missing *what the Holy Spirit knows* about the situation, and He is there as your Comforter.[47]

He is also our Wonderful Counselor.[48] Now when you don't take advantage of the Holy Spirit's prayer language, it's like going to court without an attorney to plead your case. That sounds foolish to me.

Then *praise!* Praise takes you out of the situation into the presence of God, *where all things are possible!* About then, hope is restored and joy shows up. I've read that the meaning of joy has to do with dancing and spinning around. So do a little singing, dancing and spinning around before the Lord, *in anticipation of your victory*, which you are believing is on the way and I agree with you!

In a book explaining the whole armor of God (Eph. 6:14–18), I learned how to say it in an easy to remember way, which I say every day, before I pray my Scripture pages like this: "I put on the whole armor of God, the helmet of salvation, the breastplate of righteousness, gird my loins with Truth, shod my feet with the Gospel of peace, take the shield of faith, which is able to quench all the fiery darts of the wicked one, and the sword of the Spirit, which is the Word of God; praying always with all prayer and supplication in the Spirit, watching thereunto with all perseverance and supplication for all saints." This way you start the armor from the top down.

---

[47] One who pleads another's cause, an intercessor, and advocate. *Vine's Complete Expository Dictionary*

[48] A person who gives advice as a job; . . . a lawyer. *Merriam-Webster Inc*

It's important and I do it every day by faith with confidence in the Word of God Almighty, which is final authority in my life. I have recently been remembering to say that "taking the shield of faith with which your will be able to quench all the fiery darts of the wicked one." I don't give the enemy any opportunity to attack me.

One minister has said, when you have on the armor of God, the enemy can't tell if it's you or God! So when he sees me, he sees the whole armor of God, and he doesn't want to mess with me, because I am more than a conqueror—a Believer!

That's where you have to *believe* greater (mightier) is *He that is in you than he* that is in the world. (1 John 4:4 AB) Then command the devil to get out of your life, your family, off your property, and forbid him to come back in Jesus' Name! Do this daily. Use that mighty One that is in you to protect yourself, your family and your stuff.

In seriously difficult situations or in "the combat zone", we have to cast[49] down imaginations, choose to speak the Word, refuse to faint or give up, believe the Word is working even when you can't see it or feel it, and trust God that He will *always cause you to triumph.* (2 Cor. 2:14) The battle is the Lord's[50] the Victory is ours! Take it! Remember *it has been paid for by Jesus!*

See yourself with the answer now and praise Him for it. If you shout and cheer at ball games, and other celebrations, how much more should you thank God for what He has done for you? Sing, dance and rejoice about God's love for you. "He

---

[49] In Greek it means to pluck out, drive out, expel, take or thrust out, put out, send away.

[50] 2 Chron.7:15

that spared not His own Son, but delivered Him up for us all, how shall He not with Him also freely give us all things?" (Rom. 8:32) So *continually* think about His love for you and praise Him!

[For more information on this topic get *The Believer's Authority,* Kenneth E. Hagin, *Faith Library Publications, www. rhema.org*]

These are the signs Jesus said would happen to Believers in Mark 16:17:

"And, behold, I send the promise of my Father upon you: but tarry ye in the city of Jerusalem, until ye be endued with power from on high." The MSG says, "What comes next is very important: I am sending what my Father promised to you, so stay here in the city until he arrives, until you are equipped with power from on high" (Luke 2:49).

"And with great power the apostles gave witness to the resurrection of the Lord Jesus. And great grace was upon them all" (Acts 4:33 NKJV).

"Now Stephen, full of grace (divine blessing and favor) and power (strength and ability) worked great wonders and signs (miracles) among the people" (Acts 6:8 AB).

"And the people with one accord gave heed unto those things which Philip spake, hearing and seeing the miracles which he did. For unclean spirits, crying with a loud voice, came out of many that were possessed with them: and many taken with palsies, and that were lame, were healed" (Act 8:6, 7).

"And there he found a certain man named Aeneas, which had kept his bed eight years, and was sick of the palsy. And Peter said unto him, Aeneas, Jesus the Christ maketh thee whole: arise and make thy bed. And he arose immediately" (Act 9:33, 34). So even after being paralyzed for eight years (you can imagine how he looked), the command of a Believer caused this man to rise up immediately, which was a sign of the power of Jesus' Name, *and* caused all who dwelt at Lydda and Sharon *to turn to the Lord*. That was a glorious day! Evidence that healing miracles cause people to get 'saved'.

"And there sat a certain man at Lystra, impotent in his feet, being a cripple from his mother's womb, who had never walked: This same heard Paul speak: who stedfastly beholding him, and perceiving that he had faith to be healed, said with a loud voice, Stand up straight on your feet! And he leaped and walked" (Acts 14:8–10). This man's time was well spent listening to Paul speak, which gave him *the faith* to be obedient to respond when Paul spoke to him, and *he received his miracle.*

Paul had such a strong anointing on him like Jesus, that whatever fabric was on his body could be *transferred to another* that needed healing and deliverance. It was called *virtue:* the manifestation of *His divine power* as in Mark 5:30; Luke 6:19; 8:46. "And God wrought special miracles by the hands of Paul: so that from his body were brought unto the sick handkerchiefs or aprons, and the diseases departed from them and the evil spirits went out of them" (Acts 19:11, 12). Similar to when the woman with the issue of blood touched the hem of Jesus garment.

"Finally, my brethren, be strong in the Lord and in the power of His might" (Eph. 6:10). Notice this is a charge to the church (my brethren) from Paul to not just sit there; *obey His leading,* and accomplish mighty things in His Name. We are His hands and feet on this earth to do the greater things.

Power of Agreement: "Do not be unequally yoked together with unbelievers . . . Or what part has a believer with an unbeliever" (2 Cor. 6:14a, 15b NKJV)? The apostle Paul says to avoid all associations with idolatry and *any compromising union with unbelievers.* Jesus said in Matt. 18:19: "Again I say unto you That if two of you shall agree on earth as touching any thing that they shall ask, it will be done for them by my Father in heaven."

Believe in the power of agreement, and find another Believer that will agree/harmonize with you about whatever you ask, and will continue to stand with you until it is manifested. The key is *agree and harmonize with you,* which is *the power*; that's why the enemy tries to break up this kind of union, so protect it with your prayers and authority.

I recently read testimonies of people *receiving* what they were believing for [one an incurable disease, the other with Epilepsy] when *they agreed* with another Believer according to this verse.

Can two walk together, except they be agreed?
—Amos 3:3

If the requirement of getting our request answered is finding someone that will be in agreement (in harmony with us), then an *unbeliever is out of the question.* Proverbs 12:26 NKJV says, "The righteous should choose his friends carefully, for the way of the wicked leads them astray." Finding someone that believes the Word as you do would be the best choice, otherwise it is a waste of time and can delay your answer. Psalms 119:63 says, "I am a companion of all them that fear thee, and of them that keep thy precepts."

So *don't settle for anyone less than a Believer!* I don't ask anyone to pray for me, unless I tell them specifically what I want them to agree with me about, or I believe they are more mature in the faith than I am.

"Is any sick among you? let him call for the elders of the church; and let them pray over him, anointing him with oil in the name of the Lord: And the prayer of faith shall save the sick, and the Lord shall raise him up; and if he have committed sins, they shall be forgiven him. Confess your faults one to another, and pray for another, that ye may be healed" (James 5:14–16). This prayer should be followed by the prayer Peter prayed in Acts 4:30, "By stretching forth thine hand to heal; and that signs and wonders may be done by the name of thy holy child Jesus".

If your church elders don't know how to pray "the prayer of faith" for healing, or anointing with oil according to this Scripture, don't go to them. It is better to go where Believers do this regularly and get results. *No faith—no results!*

The effective, fervent prayer of a righteous man avails much (James 5:16b–18 NKJV). The example is that even though Elijah was *just a man*, who *prayed earnestly, signs followed*, which ended the drought after three years! (1 Kings 17:1;18:41–46)

Regarding this topic, read Ephesians and underline "in Christ", "in Him", "by which He", "according to His good pleasure", "in Himself", "in Jesus" as a starter. There are a lot of these phrases of *what belongs to you through Him.*

A Hedge of Protection
Around You and Your Family

Psalm 91 is considered 'a prayer of protection', and has been reprinted and sent to our military where ever they are by some ministries. It is a good Psalm to *memorize or confess* over yourself and your loved ones *daily,* even if you can only remember a few verses. [The devil did when he tempted Jesus in the wilderness. (Matt. 4:6)]

You can print out the most important verses to you on index cards, or a confession sheet. Then begin saying them regularly, until you know them by heart. *They need to be what comes out of your mouth first in difficult or dangerous situations.*

> He shall deliver thee in six troubles:
> yea, in seven there shall no evil touch thee.
> —Job 5:19

There was a story about a woman who had been attacked after hearing a teaching on this Psalm, but couldn't remember the verse exactly, so she just said "feathers, feathers" and her assailant ran away. This refers to verse: 4 which says, "He shall cover thee with his feathers, and under his wings shalt thou trust."

Psalms 91:1–13:

> *He* that dwelleth in the secret place of the Most High shall abide under the Thou shalt not be afraid for the terror by night; nor for the arrow [mosquito] that flieth by day; nor for the

pestilence [flu] that walketh in darkness; nor for the destruction that wasteth at noonday. A thousand shall fall at thy side, and ten thousand at thy right hand; but it shall not come nigh thee. Only with thine eyes shalt thou behold and see the reward of the wicked.

Because thou hast made the Lord, which is my refuge, even the Most High, thy habitation; there shall no evil befall thee, neither shall any plague [calamity or accident] come nigh thy dwelling. For He shall give His angels charge over thee, to keep thee in all thy ways. They shall bear thee up in their hands, lest thou dash thy foot against a stone. Thou shalt tread upon the lion and adder: the young lion and the dragon shalt thou trample under feet.

This is exercising our authority over the enemy, etc. The verses beginning "Surely" through "trample under feet." in 3–13 NKJ footnote are descriptive of demonic attacks according to ancient Jewish commentators.

Psalms 91:14–16 continues:

Because he hath set his love upon me, therefore will I deliver him: I will set him on high, because he hath known my name. He shall call upon me, and I will answer him: I will be with him in trouble: I will deliver him, and honour him. With long life will I satisfy him, and shew him my salvation.

In a more detailed Psalm of circumstances when God delivered his people, it says that when "they cried out to the Lord in their trouble, and He delivered them out of their distresses" (107:6, 13, 19, 28 NKJV), because "His mercy endures forever". Notice those four verses was Old Testament before they had the Holy Spirit, *Who is the power* needed to deliver us out of the circumstance, when we speak the Word in faith.

Verse 27 says, "And are at their wits' end", which covers the many times in our lives when we don't know what to do. In verses 8,15, 21, 31 Psalms says, "Oh, that men would praise the Lord for His goodness, and for His wonderful works to the children of men!" and ends with "Whoso is wise and will observe these [things], even they shall understand the lovingkindness of the Lord."

So if you can find yourself in any of these verses where God delivered this people when they cried out to Him, then you have assurance that if He did it for an unsaved people that kept going back to idols, *He can deliver you too!,* because it is written in verse 20, "He sent His word and healed them, and delivered them from their destructions."

Remember the enemy goes about like a roaring lion, looking for someone to devour, don't let that be you or your loved ones. As the head of your household and family, *it's your responsibility* to protect them with your authority as a Believer.

Every word of God is pure:
he is a shield unto them that put their trust in him.
—Proverbs 30:5

The actress in a commercial for a security system said, "The time to think about a security system isn't after something bad has happened, *it's before!*"

When encouraging others to pray for themselves and their families, I generally add: Princess Diana didn't know when she left her home, the day she died, that she would never see her children again. Her title didn't save her nor anything else!

Don't think that just because you are a Believer, or go to church, you automatically are protected from the enemy. That's why God has given us His instruction book to show us what our part is to walk in His protection. We have not, because we ask not. (James 4:2)

Words spoken in faith supersede sight and feelings.

I believe Psalms 107 refers to the time after Joshua died, and Israel did not drive out the nations that God told them *to drive out* from the Promised Land. In Judges 2:3 the angel of the Lord said, "But they shall be as thorns in your sides, and their gods shall be a snare unto you."

They also didn't teach their children to believe in the Lord, so they reverted back to their old ways of worshiping idols, after the most recent judge died. This happened over and over again, but each time they got into trouble and distresses (thorns), they cried out to the Lord and *He delivered them, because of His love.*

Then He sent nations to prove them and *teach them war,* "To know whether they would hearken unto the commandments of the Lord, which he commanded their fathers by the hand of Moses" (Judg. 3:4). As a child, whatever you need is generally provided *in a normal family.* The child doesn't have to struggle or fight to get clothes, food or shelter, so they are not strong in that area of their life to provide for themselves. They just trust their parents to take care of them.

But we cannot continue to expect our parents to always provide for us as an adult. *We grow strong as we are tested and tried* in the real world, getting an education and job to provide for ourselves. A job, car and a home mean more to us if we have worked for them.

I believe my whole life would have been different if my parents had faithfully followed the Lord daily, and had gone to a church together that taught what I have shared in *Only Believe!* So don't rob your children of a healthy relationship with the Lord, and all that belongs to them according to the Word. *Learn and teach them by example* as Jesus did for us.

I say daily: "No weapon [curse: physically: disease, flue, virus; or spiritually: attacks of the enemy, lies, deception; poison, tornado, or tribulation] that is formed against [me] thee shall prosper; and every tongue that shall rise against [me] thee in judgment thou shalt condemn. This is the heritage of the servants of the Lord, and their righteousness is from Me, saith the Lord" (Isa. 54:17). As I think of something I missed, I add it. I recommend that you do not give the enemy any open doors, or opportunities to cause trouble also.

"Open doors" are like leaving the dandelions or weeds in your lawn, and expect that they will not spread. Dandelions have to be pulled out totally—roots and all! If you cut them down at the wrong time, you will only have hundreds more, because they sow their seeds when the wind blows, and grow stronger below the ground.

They will also take up all the space around them. If you try to kill them after they are established, then you'll be left with a lot of empty places in your lawn. "Prevention is worth a pound of cure" and causes a lot less work and money. So deal with those nasty things when they are small, new or show their ugly heads. *Don't give them any place in your life.*

> Blessed is the man who trusteth in the Lord
> and whose hope the Lord is.
> —Jeremiah 17:7

As I have said every morning, I pray over our life and day, including our protection, especially when we have places to go, things to do. One morning on the way to the athletic club, I saw three does ready to cross in front of us, and I warned my husband. One passed *very close* in front of our car anyway, and was even missed by the other car coming from the opposite direction. I believe this was our first *benefit* of the day—God's protection of us and the deer.

Since we live in Michigan and there are woods everywhere, this is the first time we have had such a close encounter with a deer. I always felt it such a treat to watch them from our apartment years ago, as they moved across the field to the other side of a busy main street. I prayed they would not get killed crossing it, and never heard a crash or saw any slain along the road after I prayed. Praise God He even cares about the deer.

New Testament Miracles

Let's begin with the angel Gabriel visiting a virgin and telling her that she would carry the Son of God—"Fear not,

Mary: for thou hast found favour with God. And, behold, thou shalt conceive in thy womb, and bring forth a son, and shalt call his name JESUS. He shall be great, and shall be called the Son of the Highest: and the Lord God shall give unto him the throne of his father David: and he shall reign over the house of Jacob for ever; and of his kingdom there shall be no end" (Luke 1:30–33, 35). "The Holy Ghost shall come upon thee, and the power of the Highest shall overshadow thee: therefore also that holy thing which shall be born of thee shall be called the Son of God." Wow! What an honor!

Think about it: the Holy Ghost just *hovered* over her and created the most precious *Life* ever, which has changed countless lives since then and He's not done yet!

Next miracle: "And, behold, thy cousin Elisabeth, she hath also conceived a son in her old age: and this is the sixth month with her, who was called barren. For with God nothing shall be impossible" (Luke 1:36, 37). Notice Gabriel said "she hath also conceived", which is *past tense*, speaking *as if Mary had already conceived*––a prophetic perfect. She then said: "be it unto me according to thy word." That's trust. Good thing for us that she *believed* the angels words!

Jairus's daughter was restored to life in Mark 5:22–24, 35–43, because he obeyed Jesus and *didn't speak a word of doubt or fear,* when He said "Be not afraid, only believe!" even when he was told she was dead! Jesus knew that fear cancels faith—they are opposites. So He warned Jairus not to go there, just trust Him—believe!

In the story about a certain nobleman whose son was near death at Capernaum, he went to Jesus to implore Him to come and heal his son. (John 4:46–54 NKJV) "Then Jesus said unto him, Except ye see signs and wonders, ye will not believe." Verse 50 says, "Go thy way; thy son liveth. And the man believed the word that Jesus had spoken unto him, and he went his way." Verse 54: "This again is the second miracle that Jesus did, when He had come out of Judea"

This is an example of *no distance with Spirit*—the son was not there in front of Jesus, the nobleman *went in faith trusting the words of Jesus,* and it was a *sign of the power* of Jesus words. Since Jesus is the same, yesterday, today and forever, we can expect the same results when we walk in faith trusting His words, that we will also see *signs following,* when someone prays the Word over us!

Jesus performed one of His miracles in the Garden of Gethsemane, when *He restored* the ear of the servant of the high priest that had been cut off in Luke 22:51: "And he touched his ear, and healed him."

"What shall we do to these men? (Peter and John had just healed the lame man at the gate Beautiful *with the Name of Jesus.*) for that indeed a notable miracle [remarkable sign] hath been done by them is manifest to all them that dwell in Jerusalem; and we cannot deny it" (Acts 4:16).

When Paul and Silas were thrown into prison, after casting out a "spirit of divination" from the slave girl that was harassing them, they began praying and singing hymns to God, which got His attention. Picture two men nearly naked, beaten with rods, and then put into the inner prison (like a crawl space) with their feet fastened in the stocks, *singing praises to God!* Those were men of faith! (Acts 16:16–25)

Then God responded with an earthquake! which caused all the prison doors to open, *and* everyone's chains to be loosed!

This breakthrough also caused the keeper of the prison to be saved along with his family, *and* be baptized! This impossible situation produced much good fruit (it was not wasted), and has been preached many times about the power of praise! God brought something really good out of the persecution of his servants, which has never been forgotten. (Acts 16:26–34)

We should all take a lesson from the birds, who early in the morning, *sing in the dark* at the top of their *voices*. Maybe that is why God takes care of the birds, because the chirping sounds so cheerful, it must be praises. Does He send them to us to get us in a good mood to begin our day, or wake us up?

"There came also a multitude out of the cities round about unto Jerusalem, bringing sick folks, and them which were vexed with unclean spirits: and they were all healed every one" (Acts 5:16). It's interesting that it says "healed" and not "delivered," which could mean the words are interchangeable.

"And God has appointed these in the church: first apostles, second prophets, third teachers, after that miracles, then gifts of healings, helps, administrations, varieties of tongues. Are all apostles? Are all prophets? Are all teachers? Are all workers of miracles?" (1 Cor.12:28,29 NKJV)[51] Notice this does not say that God appointed these gifts *for just that time*, because these are all *for the benefit of the church* to be taught, healed, and encouraged, besides providing for its continuance: helps and administrations.

"God also bearing them witness both with signs and wonders, and with divers miracles, and gifts of the Holy Ghost,

---

[51]   1 Cor. 12:10 footnote: the working of miracles is a manifestation of 'power beyond the ordinary course of natural law'. It is a divine enablement to do something that could not be done naturally.

according to His own will?" (Heb. 2:4) So it's God bearing witness with signs and wonders, etc. according to *His will,* when He feels like it or sovereignly, so He's the only one who can get the glory.

Notice these *signs, wonders and miracles* were done by the disciples *after* Jesus ascended to His father in Heaven. The Book of Acts is the story of the disciples receiving what Jesus received, in order to do what Jesus did, because He said greater works would we do. (John 14:12) It is a record of Believers doing what Jesus commissioned them to *do under the power of the Holy Spirit*—The Great Commission. He knew that if they had the Holy Spirit—Himself—they could do anything. That's why the book has been called "The Acts of the Holy Spirit."

Chapter 14

Only Believe: The Promises!

"And ye shall serve the Lord your God, and He shall bless thy bread and thy water; and I will take sickness away from the midst of thee" (Ex. 23:25). Notice that the benefit of serving the Lord is that we will be blessed with our basic needs: food, water and good health, which is lacking all over the world.

"Bless the Lord, O my soul, and forget not all His benefits: Who forgiveth all thine iniquities; Who healeth all thy diseases; Who redeemeth thy life from destruction [calamities, accidents]; Who crowneth thee with lovingkindness and tender mercies, Who satisfieth thy mouth with good things; so that thy youth is renewed like the eagle's" (Ps.103:2, 3)

Notice it says, "Who satisfies thy mouth with good things", which could mean tasty morsels, or your faith confessions re: your body or life. The rest of the verse says: "so your youth is renewed like the eagle's" (Amplified adds: strong, overcoming, soaring) Now that appeals to me, and I confess it regularly. [In *My Dreams & Goals* notebook, I have three pictures of myself: one at sixteen, one in high school, and one in my . . ., regarding those areas I want restored; and I look at these (which I have copied to my computer station), as I make my faith confessions daily.]

"And Jesus said unto the centurion, Go thy way; and as thou hast believed, so be it be done unto thee. And his servant was healed in the selfsame hour" (Matt. 8:13).

"But when Jesus heard it, He answered him, saying, Do not be afraid; [only believe] and she will be made well." (Luke 8:50; Mark 5:36 NKJV) Here Jesus is saying *all things are possible if you believe*, which is the verse I used for this book.

"And many other signs truly did Jesus in the presence of His disciples, which are not written in this book: but these are written that ye might believe that Jesus is the Christ, the Son of God, and that believing ye might have life through His Name" (John 20:30, 31).

"And Jesus looking upon them, saith, With men it is impossible, but not with God; for with God all things are possible" (Mark 10:27). *Believe it! Expect it!* Nothing is too difficult for Him to do for you!

One Miracle after Another

As I was reading one morning, I came
across 2 Chronicles 29:36,
which I dated July 18, 2009. This verse says,
"Then Hezekiah and all the people
rejoiced that God had prepared the people,
since the events took place so suddenly."
Five days later on my birthday, my husband
suggested we look into building a house!

Wow! did that make my day! I had been
<u>believing</u> God to move for years,
and even had a lot of stuff packed on
shelves in our guest room.
He had given me many, many promises and Scriptures
that had kept me going year after year, waiting
for my husband to hear from Him,
even though I talked about it a lot. You can imagine my joy!
So we talked to the builder, looked at a many
lots, chose the style of house we wanted
and did everything else prior to getting
the financing to do it.
Then we hit a wall!
The credit union where we had our CD
was the logical place to approach,
but when their Appraiser considered the
house plan, they would not approve it.
We were shocked, and couldn't believe this was happening.
I had prayed about everything, and kept following
the leading of the Holy Spirit daily.
Then the owner of the building company, who was our rep,
and a Spirit-filled <u>believer (who rarely went
out on these kind of home sales himself)</u>,
suggested we use the bank he always uses, which
is where we had our checking accounts.
So we took his advice, and they sent out their Appraiser,
who had a long impressive resume of his qualifications,
and he approved the amount of the mortgage justified!

You can imagine our joy now!
God gave us favor and made a way
where there was no way!

I can't tell you how many times I have praised the Lord for bringing us "into the land of milk and honey", where all our needs are met *as He had promised* over and over again! I have my yellow Craftsman house with teal green shutters, a window box above the garage, a seasonal flag on a pole from the porch, hanging baskets, and a prancing-horse-weather-vane on the copula over the garage roof. Very much like my dream house—finally!

* * *

"And Jesus, replying, said to them, Have faith in God [constantly]. Truly I tell you, whoever says to this mountain [insurmountable problem, hindrance, obstacle], 'Be lifted up and thrown into the sea! and does not doubt at all in his heart, but believes that what he says will take place, it will be done for him. For this reason I am telling you, whatever you ask for in prayer, believe (trust and be confident) that it is granted to you, and you will [get it] (Mark 11:22–24 AB). The NIV says: "and it will be yours."

Even though we've gone over this before, notice that it says three times "says" and only one time "believes". So Jesus emphasized *saying* was more important than believing. Shouldn't we then *say* what we want to come to pass with the words of our mouths as He did? (John 14:24b)

"Therefore I say to you, whatever things you ask [desire/demand][52] when you pray, believe that you receive [seize/

---

[52]   *See *Vine's Complete Expository Dictionary* page 40

take] them and you will have them." [So first you believe you receive when you pray—*now;* second: *then you will have it—* immediately, "in the selfsame hour" (Matt. 8:13), beginning at the time you prayed, or in the near future. *Believe, praise and receive!*]

"And whenever you stand praying, if you have anything against anyone, forgive him, that your Father in heaven may also forgive you your trespasses. But if you do not forgive, neither will your Father in heaven forgive your trespasses" (Mark 11:24–26 NKJV).

In Matthew 21:21, 22: "Jesus answered and said unto them, Verily, I say to you, If ye have faith and doubt not, ye shall not only do this which is done to the fig tree, but also if ye shall[53] say unto this mountain, Be thou removed and be thou cast into the sea, it shall be done. And all things, whatsoever ye shall ask in prayer, believing, ye shall receive".[54]

Jesus said if you follow My directions: *have faith and do not doubt*; say to the mountain: Be removed and be cast into the sea; ask in prayer believing, you will get what you ask. Then He says: "If you can believe, all things are possible to him who believes."

If you believe you receive when you prayed, *then you have it!* So count it done! *Own it!* See it, and act as if it has already come to pass in your life. We can only please God with faith.

---

53   The KJV uses the word "shall" in the place of "will" five times in this verse. "Shall" used to express simple futurity. *Merriam-Webster Inc*

54   *Receive*: Strong's #568, Phil. 15 NKJV: To receive in full, have sufficiency . . . stresses the accomplished result of the action. Matt.20–22 NKJV footnote talks about the incredible power of believing prayer authoritatively spoken in accordance with God's will and purposes.

Faith turns God loose! *Praise God as if you have it now!* Why wait? *Praise Him now,* just as if someone had given you a gift, you thank him. How much more should you thank your Healer, your Creator, your Father, *Who loves you* with an unending love, and has the ability to do whatever you asked for?

> But the tongue of the
> wise is health. —Proverbs 12:18b

Praise Delivers from Smallpox

*There is a testimony about a missionary
in a foreign country that was diagnosed
with Smallpox, and sent to a sanitarium,
because the doctors in that country
didn't know how to treat it.
In a dream she saw two baskets:
one full and the other partially full.
She asked the Lord what his meant,
and He said that the one was
full of her complaining, etc.,
and the other had only a few praises in it.
He told her if she would fill the one with
praises, she would be healed.
So she began to praise the Lord, and praise the Lord.
She praised continuously for three days and nights!
They thought she lost her mind, but was
delivered of the Smallpox instead,
and walked out of the sanitarium totally healed!*

* * *

To Martha at Lazarus's tomb, "Jesus saith unto her, Said I not unto thee, that if you wouldest believe thou shouldest see the glory of God?" (John 11:40).

"Verily, verily, I say unto you, he that believeth on Me, the works that I do shall he do also; and greater works than these shall he do; because I go unto My Father. And whatsoever ye shall askin My name, that will I do, that the Father may be glorified in the Son. If ye shall ask any thing in my name, I will do it" (John 14:12–15).

Ye have not, because ye ask not.—James 4:2

"If ye abide in Me, and My words abide in you, ye shall ask what ye will, and it shall be done unto you" (John 15:7). Jesus says abide in Me, spend time with Him—*the Way*; read the Word—*the Truth*, which is Him; next ask Him—Who is *the Life,* and then it will be done for you.

Notice Jesus repeated verse 14 with extra detail in 15:7, so it was clear to the hearer. The verses prior to this talked about believing in who He is, and His abilities through His father.

This goes with: "Ask, and it shall be given you; seek, and ye shall find; knock and it shall be opened you. For every one that asketh receiveth, and he shat seeketh findeth; and to him who knocketh it shall be opened" (Matt.7:7, 8).

"But if the Spirit of Him that raised up Jesus from the dead dwells in you, He that raised up Christ from the dead shall also quicken your mortal bodies by His Spirit that dwelleth in you" (Rom. 8:11). So since He says He will give life or "quicken" our bodies, ask Him to quicken your body, by His Spirit to agree with His Word, which says you're healed!

Quicken me after thy loving kindness
—Psalms 119: 88

"Quicken thou me according to Thy Word" (Ps.119:25b). Here's a good confession to say daily: **Holy Spirit, quicken my body, soul and spirit according to Your Word, which I have believed.**

"For the Scripture saith, Whosoever believeth on Him shall not be ashamed" (Rom.10:11).

"Now the God of hope fill you with all joy and peace in believing, that ye may abound in hope, through the power of the Holy Ghost" (Rom. 15:13). Notice it's the Holy Ghost that gives joy, peace and *hope* from God—more evidence of *His love.*

"For our light affliction [to suffer in some way], which is but for a moment, worketh for us a far more exceeding and eternal weight of glory" (2 Cor. 4:17).

Second Corinthians 4:18 AB: "Since we consider and look not to the things that are seen but to the things which are unseen [the promises of God not yet fulfilled]; for the things which are visible are temporal [subject to change] (brief and fleeting), but the things that are invisible are deathless and everlasting." When there is a bad weather forecast, I say: "I bind that up from happening, and it is subject to change in Jesus' Name!" Sometimes I agree with what the Believers are praying for in that area, also.

Doesn't this give you hope your skin is subject to change also? Especially since Jesus is coming back for "A glorious church, not having spot or wrinkle or any such thing, but that she should be holy and without blemish" (Eph. 5:27b).

> Thou art all fair, my love;
> there is no spot in thee.
> —Song 4:7

"Faith chooses to believe God's word above the evidence of the senses, knowing natural circumstances are to be kept subject to the Word of God. It is in believing God's testimony and living in agreement with it."[55] Agree with what God says about you *with tenacity:* By Whose stripes you were healed. *Refuse to be denied this Word!* because it belongs to you, and you should enjoy the benefit of it. Remember you took it by faith.

"Do not fret or have any anxiety about anything, but in every circumstance and in every thing by prayer and petition (definite requests) with thanksgiving, continue to make your wants known to God" (Phil. 4:6 AB). [Requests and wants are interchangeable depending on version.] So begin saying **"I believe You have heard my prayer/petition, and I am receiving my answers now, because You hasten to perform Your Word. Thank You Lord. Praise You, praise You!"**

Keep praising and praising. As satan listens to your praises, he will flee, because it is your *faith* talking. Remember a *sacrifice of praise:* believing and thanking God in *faith* that He hears you and that He will answer!

---

[55] NKJV: Key Lessons of Faith

> For we walk by faith . . .
> not by sight or appearance.
> —2 Corinthians 5:7 (AB)

Once again "Without faith it is impossible to please Him[56] for he that cometh to God must believe that He is", and that He is a rewarder of them that diligently seek Him." Don't take the road of least resistance—conquer! We are to *think faith, speak faith, act in faith and keep faith* until you see, or feel your answer fulfilled in the natural.

> *Faith shouts the walls down—*
> *takes Heaven by force!*

This is a great place to talk about Joshua, who was the servant of God that followed His strategy to literally *shout down* the walls of Jericho, and take *it by force* in Joshua 6. At the end of his life, after the promised lands he conquerored had been divided up, verse 21:43–45 says,

> And the Lord gave unto Israel all the land
> which he sware to give unto their fathers; and
> they possessed it, and dwelt therein. And the
> Lord gave them rest round about, according to
> all that he sware unto their fathers: and there
> stood not a man of all their enemies before
> them, the Lord delivered all their enemies into
> their hand. There failed not ought of any good

---

56 NKJV footnote says: Nothing so pleases God as a steadfast faith in all that He is and promises to do.

thing which the Lord had spoken unto the house
of Israel; all came to pass.

Joshua reminded the Israelites of this again in 23:14 when
he said: "That not one thing has failed of all the good things
which the Lord your God spoke concerning you; all have come
to pass for you, and not one word of them has failed." If God did
this for his people who were not born-again Believers, couldn't
He do this for us? So begin to say "**Not one good thing the
Lord has promised me will fail, all will come to pass. As He
did for Israel, He'll do for me, because I'm His child.**"

Hebrews 10:23 says, "Let us hold fast the profession of our
faith without wavering; (for He is faithful that promised)" James
1:17 says, "The Father of lights with whom is no variableness,
neither shadow of turning." So God is unchangeable; He always
keeps His promises!

*I refuse to be denied
what God has promised me in His Word!*

"Cast not away therefore your confidence, which hath great
recompence of reward. For ye have need of patience, that, after
ye have done the will of God, ye might receive the promise"
(Heb.10:35, 36). This could be why we don't get our prayers
answered immediately, because we wouldn't have learned
patience or endurance. God is not a "sugar daddy" or sometimes
called a "heavenly butler".

It may be you wouldn't have learned to trust Him any other
way, than if you went through the circumstance in His care.

There is no testimony without a test. So do the will of God, and *believe* for the promise or reward to come.

"Beloved, if our heart condemn us not, then have we confidence toward God. And whatsoever we [ask], we receive[57] of Him, because we keep His commandments, and do those things that are pleasing in His sight" (1 John. 3:21, 22) *Whatsoever* means of any kind or amount at all; whatever.[58] So the reward of the obedient believer, that does those things that are pleasing in God's sight, is that they can ask God for anything, according to this Scripture. That's great incentive to please Him!

MSG says, "We're able to stretch our hands out and receive what we asked for because we're doing what He said, doing what pleases Him." So we receive a reward, when we do what He leads us to do.

"And in that day ye shall [ask] Me nothing. Verily, verily, I say unto you, whatsoever ye shall [ask] the Father in My name He will give it you. Hitherto have ye asked nothing in My name: [ask], and ye shall receive, that your joy may be full" (John 16:23, 24).

"And this is the confidence that we have in Him, that if we [ask] anything according to His will, He heareth us: and if we know that He hear us, whatsoever we [ask], we know that we have the petitions that we have desired of Him" (1 John 5:14, 15). So *ask* whatsoever you desire and *believe* He heard your petition, then thank Him and praise Him as if you have it now! *Do it by faith.*

---

[57]   *receive*: acquire, . . believe, ...experience. Merriam-Webster Inc
[58]   *Merriam-Webster Inc*

As you can see Jesus has given us at least six verses to get our prayers or petitions answered, if we will just ask. He didn't say we had to beg, or stand on one foot facing east for twenty minutes. Just ask according to the Word and *believe you receive when you ask!*

If the doctor came to you and said that the disease was gone, wouldn't you be joyful and praise God? Why wait? Praise Him now in faith! Believe that your prayer is answered before symptoms leave. Don't allow symptoms to cause you to doubt God's Word!

The only reason for God's promises to you are for them to *bless you.* Claim your rights to those words as a Believer, and *refuse to be denied* the blessings that go with them. They were revealed to you by the Holy Spirit to be taken and brought into the natural by your prayer and faith. Don't let the devil rob you of your benefits, because of your complacency or ignorance of what belongs to you.

"A merry heart doeth good, like a medicine:". . . (or makes medicine even better) (Prov. 17:22 NKJV) So praise until you can laugh and sing praises to the Lord. Laugh by faith, and especially if you don't feel like it. Ha, ha, ha, ho, ho! If you keep it up, you'll end up really laughing. It has been found that laughter quickens the endorphins in the brain that trigger healing to your body. So laugh more. Watch comedies, anything light; nothing that makes you sad or cry!

Whatsoever a man soweth, that he shall he also reap (Gal. 6:7b). *This is a law* whether you are a Christian or not! So sow the Word, the seed (Luke 8:11), on healing into your mind and heart in abundance, and you will reap a harvest of healing. (Gen.8:22) Just as a farmer plants a seed in the ground to reap a plant, sow the Word (the substance)—seed—*in faith* for the things you are hoping for, and *expect a harvest*, as you water it with your praises. Praise God for it every time you think of it.

Have you ever noticed when the ground is sprinkled with grass seed, only a few blades come up? But when the seed sown is in abundance, fertilized and watered daily, you get a quick response of new grass. If you don't do the job right the first time, you'll have to do it again. So if you want an abundant harvest, don't be stingy with the seed you sow. This principle also applies to your giving.

Isaiah 55:8–11:

> For my thoughts are not your thoughts, neither are your ways my ways, saith the Lord. For as the heavens are higher than the earth, so are my ways higher than your ways, and my thoughts than your thoughts. For as the rain cometh down, and the snow from heaven, and returneth not thither, but watereth the earth, and maketh it bring forth and bud, that I may give seed to the sower, and bread to the eater; so shall my word be that goeth forth out of my mouth: it shall not return unto me void [empty], but it shall accomplish that which I please, and it shall prosper in the thing whereto I sent it.

This is the reason we must use the Word if we want to see results in our life.

How forcible are right words! —Job 6:25

So when the Lord has given you a promise, remind Him of this Scripture that: **It will not return empty to Him, but will accomplish what He has promised, and even prosper in your life**. The Action for this verse from the NKJV says: Choose to believe that God's Word is the most powerful force in the universe and act accordingly. [If the church only *believed* and did this one thing, we would see miracles everywhere daily.]

> For all the promises of God in Him are yea,
> and in Him Amen,
> unto the glory of God by us.
> —2 Corinthians 1:20

Chapter 15

Only Believe:
God is Faithful!

Isaiah 43:26 NKJV says, "Put Me in remembrance; let us contend together; state your case, that you may be acquitted." This is reminding the Lord of what He has said He would do for you: be your refuge and strength, never leave you, supply all you needs, give you wisdom, and be your Healer. I've seen a minister lift his Bible up to the Lord and say "You said right here . . ." referring to a particular Scripture.

"God is not a man, that He should lie; neither the son of man, that He should repent: hath He said, and shall He not do it? or hath He spoken, and shall He not make it good?" (Num. 23:19 NKJV: God remains true to His first intention) Hallelujah!

"And the Lord said to Moses, Has the Lord's arm been shortened? (Is the Lord's power limited?) Now you shall see whether what I say will happen to you or not" (Num.11:23 NKJV Ref. col.). The Holy Spirit has given me this verse many, times, and it has always encouraged me. Since I journal what special things happen each day, I've been able to record what He did do after that promise. I highly suggest you to write down the promises the Holy Spirit quickens to you, and then *reread* them when you need encouragement. It works!

"And said, O Lord God of Israel, there is no God like thee in heaven, nor in the earth; which keepeth covenant, and shewest mercy unto thy servants, that walk before thee with all their hearts" (2 Chron. 6:14).

"For all the promises of God in Him are Yea, and in Him Amen unto the glory of God by us" (2 Cor.1:20 NKJV) Amen: Yes, so be it. This verse gives us assurance that the thing promised by God will be done *by Jesus.* It promises us an affirmative answer through Jesus of all the promises of God in the Bible. Shouldn't this give you confidence to approach Him in your time of need?

That it might be fulfilled.
--Matthew 1:22

As I was reading one day, I began noticing how much the phrase "that it might be fulfilled" kept showing up. So far I have found fourteen Scriptures where that phrase is used in some way, and most often by Jesus.

Let's begin looking at Matthew 1:21, 22: "And she shall bring forth a Son, and thou shalt call His name **Jesus**: for He shall save His people from their sins. Now all this was done that might be fulfilled which was spoken of the Lord through the prophet".

"When he arose, he took the young child and his mother by night, and departed into Egypt; and was there until the death of Herod; that it might be fulfilled which was spoken of the Lord by the prophet, saying, Out of Egypt have I called my son" (Matt. 2:14,15).

"And he came and dwelt in a city called Nazareth: that it might be fulfilled which was spoken by the prophets, He shall be called a Nazarene" (Matt. 2:23).

Matthew 8:16,17: "When the even was come, they brought unto him many that were possessed with devils: and He cast out the spirits with his word, and healed all who were sick, that it might be fulfilled which was spoken by Esaias the prophet saying, Himself took our infirmities and bare our sicknesses."

This is one of the most important healing Scriptures to *memorize and say often*, especially if you are tormented with symptoms. Use it to control your thoughts and your body. Saying it keeps your focus on Jesus on the cross, not your symptoms, which then become lies or deception, because the Word is the Truth!

"That it might be fulfilled which was spoken by Esaias the prophet" (Matt. 12:17).

Jesus talking about praying for twelve legions of angels: "But how then shall the scriptures be fulfilled, that thus it must be? . . . But all this was done, that the scriptures of the prophets might be fulfilled" (Matt. 26:54–56). Here He is saying He is following the plan of God.

"And they crucified him, and parted his garments, casting lots; that it might be fulfilled which was spoken by the prophet, they parted my garments among them, and upon my vesture did they cast lots" (Matt. 27:35).

"I was daily with you in the temple teaching, and ye took me not: but the scripture must be fulfilled" (Mark 14:49).

"And the scripture was fulfilled, which saith, And he was numbered with the transgressors." (Mark 15:28; Isa. 53:12) The footnote in the Amplified says that "many manuscripts don't include this verse", even though it actually happened!

"For these be the days of vengeance, that all things which are written may be fulfilled" (Luke 21:22).

"And He said unto them, These are the words which I spake unto you while I was yet with you, that all things must be fulfilled which were written in the Law of Moses and the prophets and the psalms concerning Me" (Luke 24:44).

"If He called them gods, unto whom the word of God came, and the scripture cannot be broken" (John 10:35).

"I speak not of you all: I know whom I have chosen; but that the scripture may be fulfilled, He that eateth bread with me hath lifted up his heel against me" (John 13:18).

"But this cometh to pass, that the word might be fulfilled that is written in their law, They hated me without a cause" (John 15:25).

"While I was with them in the world, I kept them in thy name: those that thou gavest me I have kept; and none of them is lost, but the son of perdition; that the scripture might be fulfilled" (John 17:12).

"Jesus answered, I have told you that I am He: if therefore ye seek me, let these go their way: that the saying might be fulfilled, which He spake, Of them which thou gaveth me I have lost none" (John 18:8, 9).

"That the saying of Jesus might be fulfilled, which he spake, signifying what death he should die" (John 18:32).

"They said therefore among themselves, Let us not rend it, but cast lots for it, whose it shall be, that the scripture might be fulfilled which saith" (John 19:24).

"After this, Jesus, knowing that all things were now accomplished, that the scripture might be fulfilled, said, I thirst!"(John 19:28)

"For these things were done, that the Scripture should be fulfilled, A bone of him shall not be broken" (John 19:36).

"Men and brethren, this scripture must needs have been fulfilled, which the Holy Ghost by the mouth of David spake" (Acts 1:16).

Even Ezra 1:1 says, "Now in the first year of Cyrus king of Persia, that the word of the Lord by the mouth of Jeremiah might be fulfilled."

So from all these Scriptures we can see *if God has said it, it shall be fulfilled!* What a great promise that He repeats over and over again. I have created the acronym **SMBF**: **S**cripture **M**ust **B**e **F**ulfilled, and added it throughout my prayer sheets and faith confessions, as a reminder to God that Jesus said: "It is written" (Matt. 4:4). He promises to fulfill His Word to me, because I believe I hear my Father's voice and the voice of a stranger, I will not follow!

> My covenant will I not break,
> nor alter the thing that is gone out of my lips.
> —Psalms 89:34

So I put these two Scriptures together in a faith confession: **"It is written, By His stripes we were healed, and Scripture must be fulfilled! So thank You Lord that You are faithful to keep Your Word, and I believe I have my healing manifested now! Hallelujah!"**

* * *

"Men do not despise a thief if he steals to satisfy himself when he is hungry. Yet when he is found, he must Restore seven times [what he stole]; he must give the whole substance of his house [if necessary—to meet his fine]" (Prov. 6:30, 31 AB). This is called "The Sevenfold Return".

"For I will hasten My word to perform it" (Jer. 1:12b). The Amplified says: "I am alert and active, watching over My word to perform it." The NIV says: "for I am watching to see that My word is fulfilled." That is why it is so important to say what God says, because there is *power in consistently speaking the Word*: it changes your thinking, as it develops your faith to change the things you are speaking about. So say the Word in the face of contrary circumstances! Remember the *Word can do the same as if Jesus was right there*, because He is the Word!

Faith in God's faithfulness is *believing God will do what He has promised*, because He does not lie. "Faith is to believe what we do not see; and the reward of faith is to see what we believe." Spoken by a well known minister of the Gospel.

"But those who wait for the Lord [who expect, look for, and hope in Him] shall change and renew their strength and power; they shall lift their wings and mount up [close to God] as eagles [mount up to the sun]; they shall run and not be weary, they shall walk and not faint or become tired" (Isa. 40:31 AB)

"Every valley shall be filled, and every mountain and hill shall be brought low; and the crooked shall be made straight and rough ways shall be made smooth; and all flesh shall see the salvation of God" (Luke 3:5). The Holy Spirit has quickened this Scripture to me many times, so I confess it in faith over my life, and regarding the salvation: deliverance (of symptoms) soundness, general well-being, healing and restoration of my body. Psalms 147:15b says, "His word runneth very swiftly." So I want to use His Word to get things done!

"Submit yourselves therefore to God. Resist the devil and he will flee from you" (James 4:7). When the devil shows up with symptoms of a cold, flu or anything else, stop him right in his tracks and say: **"No devil take your weapons and flee! I don't receive your lies, get out of here, and I forbid you to come back! I'm redeemed from "the curse" for Christ became a curse for me. I am the healed protecting my health! I plead the Blood of Jesus over my body, and life in Jesus' Name! I demand my rights, which Jesus bought and paid for on the cross with His Blood!"**

She Got What She Said

A Full Gospel minister shared a testimony of a woman
with stomach cancer he visited in the hospital,
that had lost a lot of weight.
When he approached her, she said "I'm so weak,
I just can't eat, and food won't stay down."
She kept saying this until he said to her to begin saying
"I'm strong in the Lord. I have a ravenous appetite
and everything I eat stays down."
She did what he told her to do immediately,
over and over and over again
while he was there and after he left,
until she regained her weight and was restored to health.

Remember Mark 11:23 says, "But believes that those things he says will be done, he will have whatever he says." Her obedience to *say* what she needed produced it in the natural!

* * *

All scripture is given by inspiration of God,
and is profitable for doctrine, and for reproof,
for correction, for instruction in righteousness:
that the man of God may be perfect, thoroughly
furnished unto all good works (2 Tim. 3:16, 17).

[Revere God's Word very highly. Recognize its
fully divine source of inspiration. Submit to it
absolutely. NKJV Action]

If you haven't by now learned that *God loves you*, and it's His will that you be made whole, with all He has provided for you with His Name, His Word, the cross, the Blood of Jesus, His promises, His faithfulness, and His ability to do the miracles you need, then let's look at more Scriptures of His character and love.

Chapter 16

Only Believe:
He Hears You

We use our mouths for lots of things, some good, some bad; but what does the Word say we should do with them? "The word is nigh thee, even in thy mouth and in thy heart: that is, [the word of faith], which we preach; that if thou shalt confess with thy mouth the Lord Jesus and shalt believe in thine heart that God hath raised Him from the dead, thou shalt be saved. For with the heart one believes unto righteousness; and with the mouth confession is made unto salvation" (Rom.10:8–10).

This of course is the salvation Scripture, but it has a lot of words that speak of *the words of our mouths*. It is saying you have heard the preaching on the Word of faith, and it has gotten into your heart, where you believed it and received it! *So now put it into your mouth and speak it out in faith.* It's that simple.

When you believe things, don't you talk about them? Well, if you believe the Word of God when you received it, or understood it, then you need to *say it*, or *confess it*, instead of what you've been saying, which is not beneficial to your circumstances. Wrong confession shuts out the Lord, and opens the door to the enemy, besides delaying the answer you want.

Believe is written 318 times in the Bible in some form.

Do you believe by now that when you speak the Word, you are confessing the Lord Jesus? "Therefore, holy brethren, partakers of the heavenly calling, consider the Apostle[59] and High Priest of our confession, Christ Jesus" (Heb. 3:1 NKJV) Wouldn't you want the person that is hearing you speak, to have the ability to perform what you say? Well, Jesus is that One.

"We have a great High Priest Who has [already] ascended and passed through the heavens, Jesus the Son of God, let us hold fast our confession [of faith in Him]. For we do not have a High Priest Who is unable to understand and sympathize and have a shared feeling with our weaknesses and infirmities and liability to the assaults of temptation, but One Who has been tempted in every respect we are, yet without sinning. Let us then fearlessly and confidently and boldly draw near to the throne of grace (the throne of God's unmerited favor to us sinners), that we may receive mercy [for our failures] and find grace to help in good time for every need [appropriate help and well-times help, coming just when we need it]." (Heb. 4:14–16 AB).

It is said: "God is never late, but He is never early", and "There is no eleventh hour rescue He cannot perform." We know this is true and have experienced it in our own life.

That sounds like you can go unafraid to your Heavenly Father *and only receive a loving response from Him*, because you already have His mercy, grace and favor to come. He is saying with open arms and a smile "yes" before you even get there. It's like the prodigal son coming home and seeing his father coming toward him, with "compassion, and ran and

---

[59] *Apostle* means one who functions in the ministry with signs, wonders and miracles. Strong's #652, 1 Cor. 12:28

fell on his neck and kissed him." Then the father immediately called for a celebration, because the son found his way home to his family. So the father did not scold or question him about how he has been spending his time since he left. (Luke 15:20–24) That's unmerited favor, underserved blessing!

Where else can we go to where it has been written that there will be a loving person willing to help us, because He has already promised He would? There is no other person that we can confidently say would do this consistently. That's why we should never fear to go to Him, because *He loves us unconditionally!*

Second Corinthians 4:13b NKJV; "I believed and therefore I spoke, we also believe and therefore speak." And in Romans 4:17b NKJV: "God who gives life to the dead and calls those things which do not exist as though they did" as He did in Genesis 1 and created all things *by what He said.* He brought about life and order out of the void and chaos by His words. When He saw darkness, *He said what He wanted*: Light be! and it was (v.3). As His children with His Holy Spirit, shouldn't we follow His example in this and in all the other teachings of the kingdom?

God loves us so much He doesn't want anyone to say anything that will harm, or hinder His plans for us. He wants us to use His Word to bless us and our future. Jesus told one of my favorite men of God onetime years ago, "That My people are saying what they have. *Tell them from now on, they get whatever they say!*" Now that should give you the incentive to watch your words, and only say what you *believe* and want to happen in your life, because Jesus is High Priest over your confession. (Heb. 3:1)

So begin gathering the Scriptures you want God to fulfill in your life, and confess them regularly, until they are manifested or you could go to the end of *Only Believe!* and use those I have already prepared for you. Then *thank Him* that He has heard you and is bringing them to pass in the natural realm. Jesus said in John 11:41: "Father, I thank You that You have heard Me. And I know that You always hear Me." This was just before He called Lazarus to come forth out of the tomb! Next expect your miracle and praise Him for it every time you think of it.

"Death and life are in the power of the tongue, and those who love it will eat its fruit" (Prov. 18:21). NKJV footnote: To speak life is to speak God's perspective on any issue of life; to speak death is to declare life's negatives, to declare defeat, or complain constantly. So make your words agree with God's words. "Thy word is settled in heaven" (Ps.119:89).

In a movie years ago about King David, he walked this out by speaking Scriptures as he went about his day, and he was called "a man after (God's) My own heart." He is the one who defeated a giant with a sling and a stone. He not only had a sling and a stone, but years communing with the Lord as a shepherd, dealing with the attacks of a lion and a bear with ease. So when he heard about the Philistine giant that threatened the whole army of Israel, he boldly decided to offer his services to King Saul. (1 Sam.16–17:51)

Since the timing was right (he had just been anointed by the prophet Samuel as king of over Israel), he took only *his faith*, instead of the armor, which was offered him by King Saul. Next he made this faith confession: "The Lord that delivered me out of the paw of the lion, and out of the paw of the bear, He will deliver me out the hand of this Philistine" (1 Sam.17:37).

Then he prepared for the attack with his staff, five smooth stones and his sling as he went forward toward Goliath. After Goliath cursed David, he responded with: "Thou comest to me with a sword, and with a spear, and with a shield; but I come to thee in the Name of the Lord of hosts, the God of the armies of Israel, whom thou hast defied. This day will the Lord deliver thee into mine hand; and I will smite thee, and take thine head from thee; . . . that all the earth may know that there is a God in Israel. And all this assembly shall know that the Lord saveth not with sword and spear: for the battle is the Lord's, and He will give you into our hands." In verse 17:29 after he had heard about the giant and situation, David said "Is there not a cause?"

If you have *a cause* or a giant in your life, isn't it time to defeat it, stop it in its tracks, take its head off, or stop it from controlling your life? Verse 48 says, "That David hasted, and ran toward the army to meet the Philistine." He had *divine audacity,* boldness, in his trust that God would protect him, and defeat the enemy of the armies of Israel, *if he would step out.*

Next, everything happened as he said: the enemy was defeated and *God was exalted* before the Israelites, King Saul and the Philistines. Did you notice how many times he gave all the glory to God, His Name, His ability and His delivering power? He was *fully persuaded* (believed) like Abraham that *God is able, never late,* but just on time to bring him through to victory.

So when you are making faith confessions, don't just speak them into the air regarding your body. Put your hand in front of your mouth, so the words go into your ears, heart and body. Believe the Lord hears you when you pray (Ps. 38:15b), and when you speak your faith confessions. *Picture Him there with you*, not in Heaven. He says I'll never leave you nor forsake you. The Word says that He is at our right hand. (Ps.16:8)

"Who satisfieth thy mouth [your necessity and desire at your personal age and situation] with good so that your youth is renewed like the eagle's [strong, overcoming, soaring]!" (Ps. 103:5 AB)

"Call unto Me, and I will answer thee, and shew thee great and mighty things, which thou knowest not" (Jere. 33:3). So God gives you more than you ask, when you call to Him.

> For in thee, O Lord, do I hope:
> thou wilt hear, O Lord my God.
> ––Psalms 38:15

"God is not a man, that he should lie; neither the son of man, that he should repent: hath he said and shall he not do it? Or hath he spoken, and shall he not make it good?" (Num. 23:19)

Then "she [Rahab in Jericho] said, According to your words, so be it" (Josh 2:21).

"Let the weak say, 'I am strong'" (Joel 3:10).

"Jesus said to him, It is as you say" (Matt. 27:11).

"He answered and said to him, It is as you say" (Mark 15:2)

"He answered him and said, It is as you say" (Luke 23:3)

The Power of Confessing the Word

A wealthy business man, who God called
to be a powerful Evangelist,
told about a miracle that God did when a
man was given up by the doctors,
because of his physical condition. The Evangelist
had been asked by this man's pastor
to visit him in the hospital, and pray for him, which he did.
As he was about to leave, the Lord told
him to say to the patient's wife,
begin saying: "He will live and not die
and declare the works of the Lord"
over and over again. She did this diligently,
and continuously day after day.
He shortly began to get better and better, as
she <u>continued to speak those words</u>,
he was totally healed and walked out of the hospital.
The next time the Evangelist visited
that church six months later,
the man came up to the front, and gave his
testimony of the obedience of his wife
to do what the Lord told her to do:
speak the Word over him.

Chapter 17

Only Believe:
He Will Answer!

Pray is to entreat, intercede, make supplication to God. Prayer is an address (as petition) to God.[60] That's what a *Prayer of Petition* is: a formal request for something you need that requires "supernatural help", which can be anything. In this case, it would be for manifested health of your body. So you need to search the Bible for the Scriptures that fit your request, write them down, date it, and take it to your Heavenly Father, expecting Him to grant your request, because He has promised *whatever we ask in Jesus' Name He will do it.* (John 11:22)

It is similar to an attorney preparing a brief, and presenting it to the Judge with all the details that the Judge needs to know, even with the precedents that have been established before for an affirmative decision.

In our case, it is written we can "come boldly unto the throne of grace, that we may obtain mercy and find grace to help in time of need" (Heb. 4:16). So in the pattern of the Lord's Prayer, we should begin with words written of worship to our Heavenly Father, before we present our request or petition with the Scriptures that back up our requests, and those we are believing to be manifested in our life.

---

[60]   Merriam-Webster Inc; and *Strong's* #6419: See page 58 footnote

Habakkuk 2:2: "Write the vision and make it plain on tablets, that he may run who readeth it." A *vision*[61] is something you imagine. Do you have a vision of your life healthy and whole as in your youth? If not, why not? You need to see (look intently) yourself as in those pictures already healed, because all things are possible with God to him that believes!

In the story of King Hezekiah (2 Chron. 31:21 NKJV), the Bible says, "And in every work that he began in the service of the house of God, in the law and in the commandment, *to seek his God, he did it with all his heart.* So he prospered." (Emphasis added) He wanted to honor, hallow, and show God that he loved Him by doing what he believed pleased Him. He caused all of Judah to also honor Him (treat Him as Holy) by cleansing the temple and restoring the service of God in order to celebrate the Passover, as God commanded.

After he had brought back Judah to their rightful place of worshiping the Lord, a threat of an attack came from the king of Assyria. [That's just like the devil, when everything is going good, he throws a problem into your life to rob you of your peace.] So King Hezekiah (2 Kings 19:8–19) went up to the house of the Lord, and spread the letter from the king of Assyria before the Lord (brought the situation). Then *he worshiped the Lord* before he asked for His help, and ended his request that only God would get the glory out of this. Then God answered in a mighty way!

Shortly after that he was told that he was going to die of a sickness. So "he turned his face toward the wall [turning away from everything else and focused on God alone]" (2 Kings 20:2, 3) Then he prayed, and reminded God of his walk with Him

---

[61]   *Merriam-Webster Inc*

in truth and a loyal heart. "And Hezekiah wept bitterly." God's response was: "I have heard your prayer, I have seen your tears; surely I will heal you."

Think about it: the athlete that focuses on being the best golfer, runner, tennis player, or ball player studies other successful athletes, the game, how to win, and trains diligently. Paul says in 1 Corinthians 9:24, "Do you not know that those who run in a race all run, but one receives the prize? Run in such a way that you may obtain it." Verse 27, "But I discipline my body [beat—make it my slave, NIV] and bring it into subjection, lest, when I have preached to others, I myself should become disqualified". So what *they focus on they become*, because of diligent effort towards the goal or vision.

For a Christian, we discipline our body with our words of faith based on the Word. We set our face like a flint (with steadfastness) to reach the goal we see or imagine, obeying the leading of the Holy Spirit, as we walk every day.

If a person, group or ministry can go to a philanthropic organization, state or government and request a grant to meet their need of funds to reach their goal, and *not have to do anything,* besides fill out forms, how much more can we, as God's children, Who he loves, go to Him with our petition and expect Him to listen and help us?

So find the Scriptures pertaining to your need and write them out. Then begin with the words of worship you would like to say to the Lord, Who can give you the wisdom to bring your need to pass on anything! Next ask the Lord *specifically* for what you need. Remind Him what the Word says He will do, and thank Him that He has heard you and will answer. Then continue to thank Him every time you think of it, that *you believe you received the answer the first time you asked.*

And God granted him that which he requested.
—1 Chronicles 4:10

In the list of names of the family of Judah, one name is given two paragraphs and it is Jabez. It says that he was "more honourable than his brethren", which means motivated by principles of *honor.*[62] This may have been why when he asked God to bless him indeed and enlarge his territory (or border), that His hand would be with him and keep him from evil, that he would not cause pain (Because his mother had given him that name, since she bore him in pain.), that "God granted him what he requested" (1 Chron. 4:9, 10).

So pray: Bless me indeed and enlarge my territory. Your hand be with me; keep me from evil and "so it may not hurt me" (AB).

If God would grant a unsaved good man, because he asked him, how much more would He do for his children/Believers, who are reading the Word, making faith confessions, *and* believing He hears?

I learned what I have shared years ago as a Heavenly Grant, and have recorded many requests manifested—some in amazing ways! So I continue to *believe* for my Heavenly Grant, as it changes with our circumstances, and our needs being met. For an example, the Lord told me to make a list of everything I needed for our new home, and He would fill it.

---

[62] *Honor:* high moral standards of behavior. *Merriam-Webster Inc*

We have received every item on the list except two, which I continue to look for.

Led by the Holy Spirit to the Blessing

Following the leading of the Holy Spirit one day,
I stepped into a consignment shop where I
had bought a hutch for our dining room,
a gently used upholstered chair (the
perfect color) for our bedroom,
and now I found the perfect antique white,
counter chairs (the height we needed),
sitting right inside the entrance door!
They had just arrived and were a price we could afford!
In fact, <u>three of them</u> were <u>the price of</u>
<u>one new one</u> I considered ordering,
at a store that sold various kinds of these chairs, etc.

I was greatly blessed that day by following
the leading of the Holy Spirit!

* * *

I pray this for you: "May He grant you according to your heart's desire and fulfill all your plans" (Ps. 20:4, 5b AB). May the Lord fulfill all your petitions and my your plans succeed in Jesus' Name.

Remember 1 John 5:14, 15 says, "Now this is the confidence that we have in Him, that if we ask anything according to His will, He hears us. And if we know that He hears us, whatever we ask, we know that we have the [petitions] that we have asked of Him." The MSG: "That what we have asked for is as good as ours." That's why we praise Him and praise Him as if we have it. As if we own it now! You must take possession of it *when you ask*.

While my husband was working, God gave us our heart's desire many times, and we didn't have to save up or pay for the most expensive part of it (the corporation did). At the beginning of the new scheduling year, the corporation Lee worked for would ask their Senior Compliance Examiners what three states would they like to work in; then the Scheduler would do her best to work it in with the others, but we were blessed with favor, because I confessed it every day.

So when they asked Lee for his choices, he said the places we always wanted to visit were Hawaii, and Scottsdale, Arizona. That year he got both locations to work in, and I went with him, going early and paying the balance of our expenses. Since Lee had accumulated airline rewards, we used them to pay for my flight to Hawaii, which totaled <u>$30 out of pocket!</u> We liked Hawaii so much that we went back on a *Princess* cruise around the islands several years ago, using Lee's rewards to pay for our flight to Los Angeles and back. We generally went First Class, an added blessing.

> My God shall supply all your need
> according to His riches in glory by Christ Jesus.
> —Philippians 4:19

Besides that, we went to the *Holy Land Experience* in Orlando, the Branson theme park just before Christmas, and

Maine twice, all his expenses paid by the corporation, because it was in his work schedule! God can make a way to bless you too!

The last *blessing* was Scottsdale, Arizona *on our Anniversary!* (which was a light work week for him), because we wanted to see what it was like the end of January, in case we wanted to winter there after he retired. It was wonderful, and the weather was great! We even had High Tea at a quaint tea shoppe [more of the desires of my heart—I collect teapots, and drink lots of herbal tea.] in a perfect little *planned* town just north of Scottsdale called Carefree.

I had found it in the AAA book or some other advertising, because of the huge sundial, as you entered the town. Some of the streets were named Ho Hum, Easy Street, etc. The landscaping was outstanding, so we took lots of pictures on one of those beautiful sunny days.

Only God knew there was a tea shoppe—a surprise and a bonus—there that was cutesy, so we went back a second time for lunch! Did I mention Lee was walking in much Grace at that time? Imagine lots of tiny white round tables (where your knees almost touch), frills everywhere, along with everything that goes with tea, and the place filled with chattering women. I was delighted and will never forget it. Thank You Lord, for a sign of Your love!

For the eyes of the Lord are over the righteous,
and his ears are open unto their prayers.
—1 Peter 3:12a

Next comes the *standing in faith,* which develops your patience, for it to be manifested in the natural, "looking unto Jesus the Author and the finisher of our faith" (Heb. 12:2). Who is able to do it for you! You don't develop patience or constancy unless you have to wait for something. "Knowing this, that the trying of your faith worketh patience. But let patience have her perfect work, that ye may be perfect and entire, wanting nothing" (James 1:3, 4)

Once again praising God continually keeps your eyes off the symptoms [lying vanities] or contrary circumstances, and on Him to provide the answer. And "They that observe lying vanities forsake their own mercy" (Jonah 2:8). So don't let your five senses rule you, but be ruled by the truth of the Word.

Then continue to thank Him for being your Deliverer, your Protector, your Redeemer, your Healer, your Restorer, your Sustainer, your All-in-All, . . . Praise *Him in faith* that you have your healing now—*your miracle manifested,* because you believe that you received it, and *don't budge off* that confession no matter how you look or feel, because feelings lie; they are of the devil, who is the author of lies. So *resist them in Jesus' Name!* You don't have to have any symptoms, because Jesus bore them. The MSG: "He took our illnesses, and carried our diseases" (Matt. 8:17).

By him therefore
let us offer the sacrifice of praise to God continually,
that is, the fruit of our lips giving thanks to his name.
—Hebrews 13:15

In the Billy Graham telecast on his ninety-fifth birthday, they filmed scenes of a carpenter who had built a perfect cross of wood, and then nailed various sized pieces of branches all over it, till it was completely covered. Then it was dropped into a hole on a hill, and the carpenter took red paint (to resemble blood) and slathered it on the cross in various places.

Next all types of people began coming to it. This was all going on while two other people were giving their testimonies of what happened to them, when they accepted Jesus as their Savior. The finale was when all the pieces that had been attached to the cross fell to the ground!

As I thought about this later, it was a perfect progressive film of how we are delivered. Jesus is the carpenter, and those branches were the sins, sicknesses, griefs, sorrows, pains that Jesus took on Himself for us when He was nailed to the cross. The red paint was His blood shed (painted on the cross by Him—the carpenter), for us to redeem us. The pieces falling to the ground symbolized him taking them to hell, revealing a perfect, clean empty cross—it is finished! The slate is clean—the past forgiven and everything with it. "Therefore if any man be in Christ, he is a new creature: old things are passed away; behold, all things are become new" (2 Cor. 5:17).

Picture your symptoms on the cross (as those branches or pieces) falling off you to the ground, setting you free from them, because Jesus bore your sicknesses and carried your diseases for you. You don't have to have them when you believe! As I've said there is no eleventh-hour rescue He cannot perform!

Nothing is impossible to those who Believe!

Chapter 18

Only Believe:
To Receive Miracles!

King Darius gave glory to God, after Daniel was pulled out of the lion's den and said, "He delivers and rescues, and He works signs and wonders in heaven and on earth, Who has delivered Daniel from the power of the lions" (Dan. 6:27).

Jesus said: "And these signs will follow those who believe in My name they will cast out demons" (Mark 16:17).[63] Also Acts 14:3 says, "Therefore they stayed there a long time, speaking boldly in the Lord, Who was bearing witness to the word of His grace, granting signs and wonders to be done by their hands."

"And they [the eleven disciples] went forth, and preached every where, the Lord working with them and confirming the word with signs[64] following" (Mark 16:20). God proved that it was His will by backing the disciples up with supernatural phenomena.

"And Peter said unto him, Aeneas, Jesus Christ maketh thee whole: arise, and make thy bed. And he arose immediately"

---

[63] NKJV The signs, confirm the ministries of Christ's ambassadors in every generation.

[64] *Signs*, Strong's #4592, Rev. 16:14 NKJV–to describe *miracles* and *wonders*, indicating divine authority in Matt. 12:38, 39; Mark 8:11, 12.

(Acts 9:34)[65]. Through the *miracle* of restoring Dorcas back to life in Joppa, "many believed in the Lord" (Acts 9:42). So God does signs, wonders and miracles through Believers to draw people to Himself.

"Show me [a sign for good], that those who hate me may see it and be ashamed, because You, Lord, have helped me and comforted me" (Ps 86:17 NKJV)[66] Also *wonders* as signs of divine authority.

"A wondrous sign", Zech. 3:8 NKJV, Strong's #4159: A miracle, sign, token, wonder. Notice it is interchangeable with *miracle*. [Make your own signs by putting up Post It Notes with reminders to Praise, Trust, Forgive, Believe, etc.]

Without exception, miracles, signs and wonders accompanied the ministry and preaching of early church leaders. They also *prayed for miracles* in Acts 4:30, seeing them not as random, occasional events, but as worthy *evidences of God's anointing* continually glorifying Christ through the church, and therefore to be sought and welcomed.

Paul said in Romans 15:19: "In mighty signs and wonders, by the power of the Spirit of God, so that from Jerusalem and round about to Illyricum I have fully preached the gospel of Christ." Based on that pattern and gifts described in 1

---

[65] NKJV: The *miracle* was not just a marvel; it was a *sign*. *Miracle*: a unusual or wonderful event that is believed to be caused by the power of God; marvel, wonder. *Merriam- Webster Inc*

[66] *sign,* Strong's #226: a token, visible illustration, portent, ensign, signpost, *a miracle*, a mighty deed or event as in Gen.9 :12-17 the rainbow, Ex. 12:13 the blood of the Passover lamb, which are visible illustrations of something–a covenant–that cannot be seen, that is an agreement between God and His people.

Corinthians 12:9, 10, 28, 29 it seems appropriate to expect *miracles* today as well. Amen!

"Then all the multitude kept silence, and gave audience to Barnabas and Paul, declaring what miracles and wonders God had wrought among the Gentiles by them" (Acts 15:12). NKJV[67]

In the Exodus 3:20 NKJV footnote: *wonders* point to or represent things larger or more important than themselves. They are usually linked to the acts of God. This is confirmed in Psalms 77:14: "Thou art the God who doest wonders". And Psalms 136:4:"To Him who alone doeth great wonders, for His mercy endureth for ever". Also Job 9:10: "Which doeth great things past finding out; yea, wonders without number." Know that God's works are often *unfathomable* by the human mind. (NKJV Action comments)

See the story of the Angel of the Lord appearing to Manoah and his wife in Judges 13:18, 19 NKJV when He burned up the goat and grain offering, ascending in the flame of the altar! "A wondrous thing."[68]

> Blessed be the Lord God, the God of Israel,
> Who only doeth wondrous things!
> ––Psalms 72:18

God promised in Exodus 34:10b, "Before all thy people I will do marvels [wonderful acts NKJV), such as have not

---

[67] *Wonders, teras;* Strong's #5059 –*Teras* denotes extraordinary occurrences, unusual manifestations, miraculous incidents . . . acts that are so unusual they cause the observer to marvel or be in awe.

[68] Strong's #6381: To perform a miracle, marvel, wonder, or supernatural deed, that is something beyond the human ability to grasp, do, or achieve.

been done in all the earth, nor in any nation: and all the people among which thou art shall see the work of the Lord: for it is a terrible thing [awesome NKJV] that I will do with thee."

"God also bearing them witness both with signs and wonders, with divers miracles, and gifts of the Holy Ghost, according to His own will?" (Heb. 2:4)

Only believe He will do the awesome miracle you are believing Him for, and praise Him in faith for it *now*, as if you had received it in the natural, because He is able and nothing is too hard for Him! Don't stop praising and *believing* until you get your miracle!

Chapter 19

Only Believe:
You Can Stand!

"Ye shall walk in all the ways which the Lord Your God hath commanded you, that ye may live, and that it may be well with you, and that ye may prolong your days in the land which ye shall possess" (Deut. 5:33). Walking involves steps so read your Bible regularly, that's how you will *know His ways*, then *be obedient* to do what it says, so you will live long and possess the land: abundant life!

"And sought Him with their whole desire [eagerly, enthusiastic or great earnestness]; and He was found of them: and the Lord gave them rest round about" (2 Chron.15:15b). So if you eagerly pursue the Lord, He will *bless* you with peace on every side. Isn't that worth your time?

"Hope thou in God: for I shall yet praise Him, the health of my countenance, and my God" (Ps. 42:11c). So hoping in God brings the benefit of a *healthy appearance*.

When I was reading my Bible one morning, the words "So it was" stood out, which caused me to reread this story of when God told Joshua to cross over the Jordan River in Joshua 3. God gave him specific instructions of what they were to do, and what would happen.

In verse 13 He says: "And it shall come to pass, as soon as the soles of the feet of the priests who bear the ark of the Lord, the Lord of all the earth, shall rest in the waters of the Jordan, that the waters of the Jordan shall be cut off, the waters that come down from upstream, and they shall stand as a heap. So it was, <u>when the people set out</u> from their camp to cross over the Jordan . . . So the waters that went down into the Sea of the Arabah, the Salt Sea, failed, and were cut off; and the people crossed over opposite Jericho. Then the priests who bore the ark of the covenant of the Lord stood firm on dry ground in the midst of the Jordan; and all Israel crossed over on dry ground, until all the people had crossed completely over the Jordan."

Notice when the people were:

#1— *obedient* to do what the Lord told Joshua to do,

#2— *walked in faith*:

> the water in the river stopped flowing,
> stood up in a heap,
> the mud at the bottom supernaturally dried up quickly and the people crossed over *completely!*

The book of Joshua is a testimony of God being with him, as He said He would be in 1:8, 9, because we see over and over again the words "And it came to pass" or "So it was". Since the Lord said: "This book of the law shall not depart out of thy mouth; but thou shalt meditate therein day and night, that thou mayest observe to do according to all that is written therein: for then thou shalt make thy way prosperous, and then thou shalt have good success. Have not I commanded thee? Be strong and of good courage; be not afraid, neither be thou dismayed: for the Lord thy God is with thee whithersoever thou goest."

> Watch, stand fast in the faith,
> be brave, be strong.
> —1 Corinthians 16:13 NKJV

As you read the book of Joshua, God directed him what to do and he did it unafraid, smiting the kings of thirty-one nations and wiping them out, to cleanse the land. Then you read verse 11:23b: "and the land rested from war." God kept His promises to Joshua, and protected him through battle after battle (ten chapters of them), which never say he was injured or sick. He was totally committed to the Lord, was *anointed* and *faithful* to do all God called him to do.

Before he died at the age of 110, he gave God glory in verse 23:3, and charged Israel in verse 6 to "Be ye therefore very courageous to keep and to do all that is written in the book of the law of Moses, that ye turn not aside there from to the right hand or to the left".

Now since we are not under the Law, but the New Covenant, we should apply this charge to ourselves regarding the New Testament.

> It is the Spirit that quickeneth;
> the flesh profiteth nothing:
> the words that I speak unto you,
> they are spirit, and they are life.
> —John 6:63

We must keep looking, focusing on, *healing Scriptures daily*, or more often, to get the healing we need, because "For the Word of God is quick and powerful."

Isaiah 55:11AB says, "So shall My word be that goes forth from My mouth [*He has already sent it through His prophets, disciples, preachers, teachers and written it in a book in lots of translations for us. There is no excuse.]; it shall not return to Me void [without producing any effect, useless], [*when you confess it to Him] but it shall accomplish that which I please, and purpose, and it shall prosper in the thing [*situation, person] for which I sent it." (*Emphasis added)

Since God supplies all our need, He has provided Scriptures on healing, or anything else we need through His Word. With all the technology we have now, you can do a 'word search' through your concordance, computer, I Phone, etc. that already has them listed by topic and reference.

Anoint yourself to stand: "Thou anointest my head with oil; my cup runneth over" (Ps. 23:5b) "Let thy garments always be white; and let thy head lack no ointment" (Eccl. 9:8). "It shall come to pass in that day that his burden will be taken away from your shoulder, and his yoke from your neck, and the yoke will be destroyed because of the anointing oil" (Isa. 10:27). "And Moses took the anointing oil, and anointed the tabernacle and all that was therein, and sanctified them" (Lev. 8:10).[69]

Each morning when I go into my "prayer closet", I anoint myself with oil after asking God to anoint it with His Holy Spirit. There have been times when I praise and worship the Lord that I pick up what looks like an empty vial, and it produces one to three streams of oil to anoint myself! Nothing is impossible!]

---

[69] Sanctified: consecrate . . . purify. *Merriam-Webster Inc*

"This is the word of the Lord unto Zerubbabel, saying, "Not by might, nor by power, but by my spirit, saith the Lord of hosts. Who art thou, O great mountain? before Zerubbabel thou shalt become a plain" (Zech. 4:6, 7a). So expect the Holy spirit to help you with your "mountain or problem", when you command it to be flattened into a plain.

"But He answered and said, It is written, Man shall not live by bread alone, but by every Word that proceedeth from the mouth of God" (Matt. 4:4, 7, 10). Jesus emerged as the Victor when satan tempted and left Him through the power of "It is written". Satan was rendered harmless and ineffective. That's why we have to *know the Words to say* that will bring the victory! You must be determined to win and not give up! Say: "**I will not be denied my rights; they belong to me as a Believer!**"

In the Hallmark movie *The Thanksgiving House*, a young man spent fifteen years doing everything he was trained to do as a Historian, to prove that the house of a lawyer, who inherited it, was the actual site of the first Thanksgiving. He *persevered daily against all odds* from the new owner, who didn't care or believe him. Besides that, the local gossip columnist caused a lot of trouble for him, because the Post Office clerk tipped her off to any activity there; the owner's fiancé's wheeling and dealing to make money off it; and a lawsuit.

This young man *kept putting one foot in front of the other* each day, pursuing his goal of proving the site was authentic— he believed and he won! He also received the blessing of a relationship with the new owner, who decided to keep the house and live there.

My point is that reaching the desired goal is not "a piece of cake". It is not always dumped into your lap the first time you pray or make a faith confession, and I am speaking from experience. It requires diligence and perseverance! That's why I've given you so many to use, as I do.

Jesus told the fishermen, after they had spent the night fishing, to go back out and throw in their nets for a catch—*they had to work!* The boat load of fish didn't jump into their boat. They had to obey and do what He said to get the reward. Sometimes *we have to do all and <u>stand</u>, trusting God,* while listening to the Holy Spirit for what we should do next.

If you have been a Believer for a long time and doing all you know to do, **don't quit!** *Your victory is just ahead of you!* God wants you to develop into such a strong, confident Believer that you can help others, because you have been there, and *know* what they are going through. Some things you can't learn unless you *go through them.* This time of testing, stretching, and standing develops our faith and causes us to grow in our trust for God, our Father, like no other way. You don't grow by leaps and bounds, but by step by step; sometimes when you don't see or feel anything there except God's promise to you.

> My brethren, count it all joy when ye
> fall into divers temptations;
> knowing this, that the trying of your faith worketh patience.
> But let patience have her perfect work,
> that ye may be perfect and entire, wanting nothing.
> —James 1:2-4

In a Harrison Ford movie (*Indiana Jones*), he has to get from one side of to the other with nothing in between! Since he had to do something, he thought then he stepped out *in faith*, and a bridge appeared miraculously. Jesus is our bridge and He will be there when you trust Him completely.

When you need a boost to keep you going read *Take It by Force* by Judy Jacobs, Charisma House; or *The Intensity of Your Desires* by Carolyn Savelle, Jerry Savelle Publications. I've read these several times and they always encourage me.

Recently when I was peeling a big, thick-skinned orange, I thought to myself that even though it was difficult to peel, the delicious juicy sweet fruit inside was worth the work. So keep standing and don't give up, there is a reward!

A well known leader in Christian Broadcasting said (after returning home from his final stay at the hospital) that he asked God "Why do You wait till I've gone under three times, before You rescue me?" He said "So you have no doubt that it was Me."

Chapter 20

Only Believe: He is Peace

"A sound heart[70] is the life to the flesh: and envy the rottenness of the bones" (Prov. 14:30)

"His name shall be called Wonderful, Counselor, Mighty God, The Everlasting Father, The Prince of Peace" (Isa. 9:6). Heaven on earth.

"You will keep him in perfect peace[71], whose mind[72] is stayed on You, because he trusts in You. Trust in the Lord forever, for in Yah, the Lord, is everlasting strength"[73] (Isa.26:3, 4 NKJ).

> The Lord is my shepherd; I shall not want [lack].
> He makes me to lie down in green pastures;
> He leads me beside the still waters.
> He restores my soul;

---

70 *sound heart* –A tranquil mind brings good physical health. NKJV footnote

71 True <u>peace</u> involves complete fellowship with God and right relations with others. It has more to do with character and attitude than outward circumstances. Jere. 6:14 NKJV foot.

72 The word translated *mind* means "creative imagination". Isaiah's thought is that he whose creative imagination, the seat of plans and ideas, is firmly founded on the eternal Lord, will enjoy *Shalom* in all its implications. NKJV

73 Rock of Ages, NKJV

He leads me in the paths of righteousness
for His name's sake.
Yea, though I walk through the
valley of the shadow of death,
I will fear no evil; for You are with me;
Your rod and Your staff, they comfort me.
You prepare a table before me
in the presence of my enemies;
You anoint my head with oil; my cup runs over.[74]
Surely goodness and mercy[75]
follow me all the days of my life
And I will dwell in the house of the Lord forever.
—Psalms 23

David wrote this well known 23rd Psalm that talks about the *Lord as our Shepherd*, which is filled with promises, peace and comfort for this life.

I heard a testimony of a man with cancer, who was told to see a wise Hebrew man in Israel, that told him to *meditate, feed on* and *confess daily* the 23rd Psalm, which he did and it healed him! In this world of stress, could it have been that he needed to spend time with the Prince of Peace, our Shepherd? Sounds like a good plan to restore our spirit, soul and body.

For I know the thoughts that I think toward you . . .
Thoughts of peace and not of evil
to give you a future and a hope.
—Jeremiah 29:11 NKJV

---

[74] This act shows favor and excellent hospitality. NKJV footnote
[75] Hebrew *chesed* is the unfailing, steadfast covenant love of God. This lovingkindness is similar to the NT word 'Grace'. NKJV footnote

"Behold, on the mountains the feet of him who brings good tidings, who proclaims peace![76] O Judah, keep your appointed feasts, perform your vows. For the wicked one (one of Belial) shall no more pass through you; he is utterly cut off" (Nah.1:15 NKJV).[77] Since the thief or enemy comes to kill, steal and destroy, **I claim he is utterly cut off from my life 24/7 in Jesus' Name!** A good confession to say every day.

"I will both lie down in peace, and sleep; for You alone, O Lord, make me dwell in safety" (Ps. 4:8 NKJ) So just fall back into His everlasting arms (Deut. 33:27), imagining that He is holding you and no evil can befall you. Just let His *peace overtake you.*

Since it is written that we have the mind of Christ, and He is not worried, but peaceful, shouldn't we seek His mind and thoughts for our situations, so we can have that same peace? And when thoughts come that would disturb that *peace*, cast them down and bring them into obedience to Christ—to what He would do or say. (2 Cor. 10:4, 5) Then *purposely* take no thought saying (Matt. 6:31). Because *if we refuse to say the thought*, then it is unborn, which will stop it from coming to pass. "So the curse causeless shall not come" (Prov. 26:2).

You are in charge of your thoughts and desires. So if they don't agree with what Jesus would think or desire, say: **"That's not my thought."** and cast it down. Don't let any unclean thought continue in your mind; it only leads to

---

[76] *Peace* in this verse refers to shalom; Strong's #7965: completeness, tranquility, perfectness, fullness, rest, harmony; the absence of agitation or discord.

[77] The message is one of deliverance from the [oppression of the enemy]. NKJV footnote

trouble. "This I say then, Walk in the Spirit, and ye shall not fulfil the lust of the flesh" (Gal. 5:16). Walking in the Spirit leads to Peace.

"The Lord will give (unyielding and impenetrable) strength to His people; the Lord will bless His people with peace" (Ps. 29:11AB). Confirmation of the meaning of *peace*—Jesus as Prince of Peace gives peace to those who call upon Him for personal salvation. (Luke 1:79 NKJV, Strong's #1515)

"Peace I leave with you, My peace I give unto you: not as the world giveth, give I unto you. Let not your heart be troubled, neither let it be afraid" (John 14:27). There may be times when the Holy Spirit brings this Scripture to your remembrance, so stop and receive His *peace*, because He already knows the future, so don't be afraid—*Only Believe!*—trust Him! Keep focused on Him and praise Him He's taking care of it, then obey what He is telling you to do.

"Be anxious for nothing, but in everything by prayer and supplication[78] with thanksgiving, let your requests be made known to God; and the peace of God, which surpasses all understanding, will guard your hearts and minds through Christ Jesus" (Phil. 4:6, 7). NKJV footnote: Prayer and peace are closely connected. One who entrusts cares to Christ, instead of fretting over them, will experience the peace of God to guard him from nagging anxiety.

---

[78] *Supplication* is more than petitioning, but suggests an intensity of earnestness in extended prayer . . . to fully transfer the burden of one's soul into God's hands. NKJV footnote

And let the peace of God rule in your hearts,
to which also ye were called in one body;
and be thankful.
—Colossians 3:15

"Grace and peace be multiplied unto you through the knowledge of God, and of Jesus our Lord" (2 Peter 1:2) NKJV footnote: Peter's message is that true knowledge is found in the God of Christ and the Scriptures. Amen!

Be still and know that He is God [79]
and He is faithful . . .

---

[79]   Chorus of song: Psalm 46:10a

Sleep & Peace

I take my place of rest in the secret place
of the Most High God. Ps. 91:1
The sleep of a laboring man is sweet. Eccl. 5:12
Yea, thou shalt lie down, and thy
sleep shall be sweet. Prov. 3:24
For the Lord will pour out on me the
spirit of deep sleep. Isa. 29:10
I declare I will both lie down in peace and sleep. Ps. 4:8
He will quiet me with His love. Zeph. 3:17b
For so, He gives His beloved sleep. Ps. 127:2
You will keep me in perfect peace whose
mind is stayed upon You. Isa. 26:3
And in this place I will give peace says the Lord. Hag. 2:9
My people will dwell in a peaceful
habitation in secure dwellings
and in quiet resting places. Isa. 32:18
When I sleep, I get well. For those who sleep, sleep at night.
John 11:12; I Thess. 5:7
And the peace of God, which surpasses all understanding,
will guard your hearts and minds
through Christ Jesus. Phil. 4:7
Grace be to you and peace from God our Father,
and from the Lord Jesus Christ. 2 Cor. 1:3

In Conclusion:

When the Lord gave me a word "Acceleration", I discovered it had to do with writing *Only Believe!* now. I had started it several years ago, when He first put this idea into my spirit, but I got sidetracked with the building and finishing of our new house. The main reason was for my own healing, as I had many symptoms that I knew didn't agree with the Word that says "by Whose stripes ye were healed."

The attacks to my body got worse as I pressed forward with this book, like the day my left wrist mysteriously received a sharp debilitating pain, as I turned to wash my hands on our way to the athletic club. The pain was so bad I couldn't move it, because I thought it was broken. When my husband came down from upstairs and saw me crying, he knew something was seriously wrong, as I have a high tolerance of pain. So fearing that he could worsen the situation by trying to get me to the hospital himself, he called an ambulance. Long story short, they couldn't find anything, but sent me home with a pain killer and a brace.

Regarding attacks: If someone was going to write a book, where would be the best place to hinder it from being written? The wrist.

For I will not dare to speak of any of those things
which Christ has not accomplished through me.
—Romans 15:18 NKJV

Also during this time I had several nasty UTIs, many canker sores, a short-lived cold attack, a wart-like growth on my finger flare-up, constant insomnia bouts, a burning in my lower arms, an allergy to something that caused my eyes to water and burn the skin around them, besides back and knee pain, and other uncomfortable symptoms. Each of these I dealt with as I have written in *Only Believe!*, besides anything else I could do in the natural, continually speaking Scriptures, doing spiritual warfare, praising God and standing on the promises with all my might at times!

The Blood of Miracles

Many times the only thing that changed the situation was confessing *the Blood of Jesus* over and over again, until the pain ceased and there was restoration. If I had not done this in faith the first time, I would not have been able to trust it the many other times the symptoms showed up after that, because fear and discomfort was banging at my door big time! I had to quickly say *the Blood of Jesus* over and over again until there was relief, and my body conformed to the Word.

So if *the Blood of Jesus* stopped the circumstances, then it was *the lies of the enemy* that was causing it, which meant it was a *deception*. It was a demonic symptom, so I used spiritual warfare to protect myself—*the Blood of Jesus*, which the enemy hates, because he was defeated by it at [the cross] and when Jesus rose from the dead, thereby *conquering death and the fear of it!* Hallelujah!

Having disarmed principalities and powers,
He made a public spectacle of them,
triumphing over them in it. [the cross]
—Colossians 2:15 NKJV

This is why *you must know* these things and *believe them*, so when the time comes to protect yourself, you will have the *faith* to know what to do and act. You cannot say "By the same Blood of Jesus that protected Jamie Dershem, I claim for me now." (Similar to the verse where the men said, who were doing an exorcism, "by the same Jesus Paul preaches" (Acts 19:13 NKJV).

You have to have: *faith in the Blood, its protection, and its delivering power without a doubt or wavering!* The devil doesn't play games. He's serious, so *you must be more serious, determined, fearless, and unrelenting!* **You must Believe utterly!** Determine now that there is no turning back, because you have nothing to go back to. You have nothing to lose going forward but Victory!

So begin now practicing with the circumstances in your life, as you pray using the Blood of Jesus to protect yourself, your family, your home (when a violent storm is forecasted), vehicles, your business, or anything else, because the devil is killing, stealing and destroying every day. You don't want to be on CBS: *Your World in 90 Seconds* tomorrow.

I had a late morning dream where I saw people in prison. It was a large room with only space up high on the walls to get out. I noticed Christians in this room. As I thought about this, I remembered all the times I told people: "If you are not actively moving forward, you will fall back." People are so caught up in their distractions: sports, social activities, families, work and complacency, that they don't think they have time to spend with the Lord, so they become weak and are taken over by their fears, which leads to addictions, drugs, alcohol, etc. they think will help them.

It's just like dandelions and weeds, if you give them an inch, they will take over the whole yard. You can't cut them down; they get stronger. They have to be dug out by the roots, or you have to put on a pre-emergent weed killer on in the spring, *before they show up.* Be proactive, and don't let distractions steal your time with God daily.

God has trained and anointed prophets, apostles, pastors, teachers (gifted people) to take us through the difficult places and times in our lives, but *we must seek them out* as Saul sought the Seer, Samuel, to find the lost donkeys, looking everywhere. We all have the same twenty-four hours. How will you spend yours?

> I would have you wise unto that which is good,
> and simple concerning evil.
> —Romans 16:19b

If you don't spend your time wisely now and practice what you have learned, you won't have the faith when something serious happens in your life. Don't be foolish like the people who go to events, thinking that nothing will happen to them, and they are caught in a fire, a multi-car accident, blinding snow storm, or near a location where a person is shooting into the crowd. The people at the Boston Marathon bombing in 2013 had no idea their lives would be changed forever that day.

Remember, the devil walks about like a roaring lion seeking whom he may devour, and he will use anyone, who opens the door to him to do his work. It's kind of like those insects that appear crawling along the baseboard or across the floor suddenly, when we think our houses are airtight. How do they get in? Generally on us or a wee small opening we don't see. Well zap "those wee small" thoughts, attacks, and symptoms at the first sign of them as you do those insects. A wise man prepares his way: *pray ahead of time* and protect yourself and your family.

Door openers are anything that are not "true, right, lovely or of good report." A list would include bars, casinos, pornography, illegal drugs, violent video games, PG 13+ movies (or worse), horoscopes, Halloween (my pet peeve), etc. In fact now, these are some of the ways that victims are pulled into Human Trafficking, which takes lives, here and around the world. So don't stick your hand into the devil's territory; he'll take the whole arm and your life too!

Behold, the fear of the Lord, that is *wisdom*;
and to depart from evil is *understanding*.
—Job 28:28 (Emphasis added)

Re: Halloween, why would you teach young children to dress up and threaten a home owner, if they don't give them candy, which causes tooth decay, obesity, diabetes, and hyperactivity? Besides it's the devil's night through satanic groups, who perform sacrifices of animals, or anything else they can capture. *It is not an innocent holiday.*

Look around at all the gruesome costumes and masks that are in the stores. Why? You can have a costume party anytime of the year for a fun reason, instead of cooperating with the devil's night. Don't get involved!

You who love the Lord, hate evil!
—Psalms 97:10a NKJV

Ever since 9/11, we have been robbed of our rights, our privacy, our peace, and much more, because of those who are under the control of the devil to steal, kill and destroy life, as we knew it. Why is it necessary to create violent, horrific movies or costumes to cause more fear in our children and our lives? *Where there is fear, there is no faith or peace.*

Blessed be God,
even the Father of our Lord Jesus Christ,
the Father of mercies, and God of all comfort;
who comforteth us in all our tribulation,
that we may be able to comfort them
which are in any trouble,
by the comfort wherewith we ourselves
are comforted of God.
—2 Corinthians 1:3, 4

Since I've done all the work and given you the Scriptures to *Believe* and stand on, now it's your responsibility to do your part and act on what you have learned.

Think: What would Jesus do? Which side are you on? *Get on God's side.* Go out and teach what you have learned and heal the sick. Do the works of *Jesus!*

Now may the God of hope
fill you with all joy and peace
in believing
that you may abound in hope
by the power of the Holy Spirit.
—Romans 15:13NKJV

Believe and get the blessings!

Meditate on these
Scriptures, Definitions and Instructions:

Read out loud to yourself, so you see the Word–**Jesus**, hear the Word–**Jesus**, because "Faith comes by hearing, and hearing by the Word of God." Get the Word–**Jesus**, into your heart. "For with the heart one believes unto righteousness, and with the mouth confession is made unto salvation" (Rom.10:10 NKJ). Verse 9: If you confess with your mouth the Lord Jesus and believe in your heart . . . you will be saved. Verse 11: "Whoever believes on Him will not be put to shame."

If you are not making *faith confessions*, the world will influence your life and speech; then you'll get what you say, instead of what you want.

Gen. 17:1: "I am Almighty God" (Hebrew: El Shaddai) The NKJV: El Shaddai whose root emphasizes God's might over against the frailty of man . . . in situations where people are hard- pressed and need assurance.

Gen. 22:14 AB: "The Lord Will Provide" (Jehovah-Jireh KJV). Phil. 4:19: "And my God shall supply all your need according to His riches in glory by Christ Jesus."

Deut. 7:15: "And the Lord will take away from thee all sickness".

Deut. 8:3 NKJV: "Man shall not live by bread alone; but by every word that proceeds from the mouth of the Lord."

"Outstretched arm" is used of God's power
to deliver, to punish or to destroy.
Jere. 6:12 NKJV footnote.

Deut. 9:26a: "Which thou hast redeemed through thy greatness, which thou hast brought forth out of Egypt with a mighty hand." Isa.50:2: "Is my hand shortened at all that it cannot redeem? or have I no power to deliver?" Jere.32:17AB: "You have made the heavens and the earth by Your great power and outstretched arm. There is nothing too hard or too wonderful for You!" Verse 21b: "With a strong hand and an outstretched arm, and with great terror." Ps. 60:5: "That thy beloved may be delivered; save with thy right hand, and hear me."

1 Chron. 23:30: "And to stand every morning to thank and praise the Lord, and likewise at even".

Ps. 27:14: "Wait on the Lord: be of good courage, and he shall strengthen thine heart: wait, I say, on the Lord."

Ps.100:4: "Enter into His gates with thanksgiving, and into His courts with praise: be thankful unto Him and bless His name." Look up Scriptures on *Praise*, write them out to use in your times of thanksgiving.

Ps.107:20: "He sent his Word, and healed them, and delivered them from their destructions."

Prov. 4:13: "Take fast hold of instruction; let not go; keep her, for she is thy life."

Prov. 4:20–22 AB: "My son, attend to my words; consent and submit to my sayings. Let them not depart from your eyes; keep them in the center of your heart. For they are life to those that find them, healing and health to all their flesh." So if you want life and health, keep your eyes focused on the Word daily.

Prov. 12:18: "But the tongue of the wise is health."

Prov. 17:22: "A merry heart doeth good like a medicine: but a broken spirit drieth the bones."

Isa. 42:22 NKJV: "But this is a people robbed and plundered . . . no one says "Restore!" So cry out Restore! RESTORE! Prov. 6:31 paraphrased: when the thief is found he has to *restore sevenfold.*

Jere. 17:14: "Heal me, O Lord, and I shall be healed; save me, and I shall be saved, for thou art my praise."

Jere. 30:17:"For I will restore health unto thee, and I will heal thee of thy wounds, saith the Lord."

Matt.6:10: "Thy kingdom come. Thy will be done in earth, as it is in heaven." We will be perfect in Heaven, so we want that same wholeness on earth while we are alive.

Matt.16:19 AB: "I will give you the keys of the kingdom of heaven; and whatever you shall bind (declare to be improper and unlawful) on earth must be what is already bound in heaven; and whatever you loose (declare lawful) on earth must be what is already loosed in heaven." NKJV

Mark 6:56: "They laid the sick in the streets, and besought Him that they might touch if it were but the border of His garment [the finished work] and as many as touched Him were made whole." Those that were brought to the feet of Jesus received.

Luke 4:4: "It is written". . . *Speak what is written* regarding your health, and everything else.

Luke 7:21 NKJV: "And that very hour He cured many of infirmities [illnesses], afflictions, and evil spirits; and to many blind He gave sight."

Luke 7:50: "Thy faith hath saved thee; go in peace."

Luke 8:2: "And certain women, which had been healed of evil spirits and infirmities."

Luke 8:15 NKJV: "But the ones that fell on the good ground are those who, having heard the word with a noble and good heart, keep it and bear fruit with patience."

Luke 9:11c: "And healed them that had need of healing."

Luke 24:38, 39: "And He said unto them, Why are ye troubled? and why do thoughts arise in your hearts? Behold my hands and my feet, that it is I myself: handle me, and see; for a spirit hath not flesh and bones, as you see I have." Picture the holes in His hands and feet as proof of what He did for you!

John 6:2: "Then a great multitude followed Him, because they saw His miracles which He which He did on them who were diseased."

John 10:10: "The thief cometh not, but for to steal and to kill, and to destroy. I am come that they may have life, and that they might have it more abundantly."

John 11:12 NKJV: "Then His disciples said, Lord, if he sleeps he will get well."

John 15:7: "If ye abide in Me, and My words abide in you, ye shall ask what ye will, and it shall be done unto you."

Acts 28:5: "And he shook off the beast (viper) into the fire, and felt no harm." *Shake off* _____

2 Cor. 13:1b: "In the mouth of two or three witnesses shall every word be established."

Gal. 3:5 NKJV: "He Who supplies the Spirit to you and works miracles among you, does He do it by the works of the law, or by the hearing of faith?" Heb. 11:6: "Without faith it is impossible to please Him" *By faith call* "those things which do not exist as though they did" (Rom.4:17c NKJV)

Phil. 4:8 NKJV: "Finally, brethren, whatsoever things are true, whatsoever things are honest, whatsoever things are just, whatsoever things are pure, whatsoever things are lovely, whatsoever things are of good report; if there be any praise, think on these things."—Jesus!

Heb. 1:3: "And upholding all things by the word of His power"—Jesus!

Heb. 3:1 NKJV: "Consider the Apostle and High Priest of our confession, Christ Jesus". *Make faith confessions of what you want out loud* so He can hear you.

James 2: 20: "Faith without works is dead?" *So step out, do something!*

James 3:2: "If any man offend not in word, the same is a perfect man, and able also to bridle the whole body." So *think before you speak*— bridle your tongue.

Rev. 5:9c, 10 NKJV: "And have redeemed us to God by Your blood out of every tribe and tongue and people and nation, and have made us kings and priests to our God; and we shall reign on the earth." Footnote: As a royal priesthood the saints reign now with Christ on the earth by their worship, their prayers, and their witness in word and deed.

Rev.12:11: "And they overcame him by the blood of the Lamb and by the word of their testimony."

If this book has been a blessing to you in some way, contact me at inoljcon@hotmail.com.

Only Believe: It is as You Say!

(These faith confessions are based on the Scriptures listed.)

Praise You, Lord, You are my Savior, Deliverer, Healer, Redeemer, Restorer, Prince of Peace, King of Kings, Lord of Lords, You are my Breakthrough, praise You, praise You . . .

You are my Shepherd; I shall not want. Goodness and mercy shall follow me all the days of my life and overtake me! I shall be BLESSED above all peoples. Thank You *Jesus for life in abundance to the full till it overflows.* Ps 23:1, 6 NKJ; Dt.7:14 NKJ; Jn 10:10b AB

Because I delight myself in You, *You give me the desires of my heart.* "Every valley shall be filled, and every mountain and hill brought low; and the crooked places shall be made straight and rough ways smooth; and all flesh shall see the salvation of God." Ps 37:4 NKJ; Lk 4:4; 3:5, 6

"Blessings are on the head of the righteous." *I have the mind of Christ.* Pr 10:6 NKJ; 1 Co 2:16b

Praise You for blessing our bread and water, and taking sickness away from the midst of us and fulfilling the number of my days in health. *I am healthy! I am strong!* Ex 23:25, 26 NKJ; Jl 3:10

Thank You Jesus for taking my infirmities, and bearing away my dis-eases. You are the Lord Who heals me! With Your stripes I am healed! Mt 8:17 NKJ; Ex 15:26 AB.; Is 53:5; Ex 23:26 NKJ; SMBF

"I cried out to You, and You healed me." So I am walking "within my house with a perfect heart" 24/7. Ps 30:2 NKJ; 1 Pe 2:24; Ps101:2c

Praise You Lord, You give power to the weak, and to those who have no might You increase strength. And because I wait/hope & expect You Lord, *You renew my strength*; I shall mount up with wings like eagles, I shall run and not be weary, walk and not faint or become tired. "I can do all things through Christ Who strengthens me." I am "strong in the Lord and the power of His might!" *I am more than a conqueror!* I am "His workmanship recreated in Christ Jesus" "As He is, so are we in this world." "For we are members of His body, of His flesh and of His bones." Quicken me according to this word. Is 40:29, 31 NKJ; Php 4:13; Eph 6:10; Ro 8:37; Eph 2:10; 1Jn 4:17b; Eph 5:30; Ps 119:154

I put on the whole armor of God, the helmet of salvation, the breastplate of righteousness, gird my loins with Truth, shod my feet with the Gospel of peace, take the shield of faith, which is able to quench all the fiery darts of the wicked one, and the sword of the Spirit, which is the Word of God; praying always with all prayer and supplication in the Spirit, watching thereunto with all perseverance and supplication for all saints. Eph 6:14-17

You are my refuge and my fortress; *my God in Whom I trust,* so no evil or accident shall befall me, nor any plague: cold, flue, virus, or calamity come near my body, car or dwelling. No *weapon:* disease, salmonella, fear, lie, deception, symptom, insect, or *curse of any kind formed against me shall prosper!* Ps 91:2, 9, 10 NKJ; Is 54:17 SMBF

I command you spirit of death and hell, to take your weapons and flee! *The wicked one shall no more pass through me; he is utterly cut off in Jesus' Name!* I believe I'm redeemed from the curse of the law and *every curse since the book of the law! I plead the Blood of Jesus over my body* from the top of my head to the souls of my feet in Jesus' Name! Na 1:15c; Ga 3:13, Dt 28:61

For You, Lord will help me, for with You nothing will be impossible. There is nothing too hard or too wonderful for You. *For with You all things are possible!* Is 50:7 NKJ; Lk 1:37 NKJ; Je 32:17 AB, Mk 10:27

Because I *believe* on You I will not be put to shame in my believing. Now thanks be to God, Who always causes us to triumph in Christ. Ro 10:11 NKJ; 2 Co 2:14 SMBF

"The effective, fervent prayer of a righteous man avails much." I declare You're doing superabundantly, far over and above all that I [dare] ask or think [infinitely beyond my highest prayers, desires, thoughts, hopes, or dreams]. Thank You Lord! Jas 5:16 NJKJ; Eph 3:20 AB

"I believed and therefore I spoke." This is the truth, and "the truth makes me free" of pain, discomfort and disease. 2 Co 4:13 NKJ; Jn 8: 32 SMBF

I freely forgive and release the Grace and Mercy of God to all institutions, organizations, corporations, persons and everyone else in my life, in Jesus' Name. I loose and let go of all erroneous beliefs, ideas, judgments, misplaced anger, bitterness, resentment and criticism. I let go and let God's LOVE do its perfect work in me, through me and for me: spirit, soul, body, and affairs. I declare *divine order* is now established, and I give thanks that Shalom now reigns supreme in me and my world. Ga 3:13, Dt 28:61

I take my place of *rest* in the secret place of the *Most High God.* "I will both lie down in peace, and sleep; and my sleep will be sweet." I will wake up refreshed and healed 365 days a year! I have declared these words, and they shall be established. Ps 91:1; 4:8 NKJ; Pr 3:24; Jb 22:28 NKJ

I *believe I received my deliverance, healing and restoration,* because with His stripes we were healed! My inward and outward man is RENEWED by the finished work of Jesus on the cross. 1 Pe 2:24; 2 Co 4:16

Praise You Lord, You are faithful to keep Your Word. You hasten to perform it. Thank You Jesus, I believe You hear my faith confessions. I am redeemed, delivered, healed and restored to perfect health now! *It's so good to be HEALED!* It is as I SAY! Jr 1:12

"Father, I thank You that You have heard me and I know You always hear me." Jn 11:41, 42 NKJ

"Let it be it unto me according to your Word." Lk 1:38b NKJ

Other References & Contributors:

By permission. From *Merriam-Webster's Collegiate ®
Dictionary,* 11ᵗʰ Edition © 2014 by Merriam- Webster, Inc.
(www.Merriam-Webster.com).

Strong's Exhaustive Concordance, James Strong, LL.D, S.T.D.,
T Nelson Pub. 1995

Vine's Complete Expository Dictionary, W. E. Vine, Merrill
F. Unger, William White, Jr. © 1984, 1996, Thomas Nelson,
Nashville, Tennessee. All rights reserved. Used by permission.

Nathaniel M Van Cleave, Special Conf. Speaker/Faculty,
Spanish Bible College, Montebello, CA

Roy Edmund Hayden, Professor of Old Testament, *Oral Roberts
Univ.*, Tulsa, OK

Jack W Hayford, Senior Pastor, *The Church On the Way,* Van
Nuys, CA; Editor *Spirit Filled Life Bible*

Charles V Simpson, General Overseer/Bible Teacher, *Covenant
Church*, Mobile, AL

Recommended books:

365 Days of Healing, Mark Brazee, Harrison House 1999

Christ the Healer, F.F. Bosworth, Revell (Baker Book House) 1973

Faith and Confession, Charles Capps, Capps Publishing 1987

God's Word for Your Healing, Harrison House 1993

Healing the Sick, T.L.Osborn, Harrison House 1951

His Healing Power, Lillian B.Yeomans, M.D., Harrison House 2003

How to Receive Communion, Kenneth Copeland, Kenneth Copeland Publications 1982

It's All About Jesus Bible (NKJV), Thomas Nelson 2004 (215 names of Jesus)

Keys to Receiving God's Miracles, E.W. Kenyon & Don Gossett, Whitaker House 2011

Scripture Confessions for Healing, Harrison House 2007

Take It By Force, Judy Jacobs, Charisma House 2005

The Meal That Heals, Perry Stone, Charisma House 2008

The Passion of the Christ, Tyndale 2004

The Untapped Power of Praise, Kenneth Hagin Jr., Faith Library Publications 1990

The Word, The Name, The Blood, Joyce Meyer, Faith Words 1995

Acknowledgments:

For my husband, Lee, who bailed me out over and over again, as I was writing *Only Believe!* and couldn't figure out how to do a variety of computer procedures. Especially the time I looked at the screen and everything I could see was *italicized!* Help!

Then there were the many times he protected *Only Believe!* by saving it on a flash drive, and reminding me to click "save" whenever I walked away or stopped for some reason.

He also did many things around the house that freed me up to study and write. And finally, I thank him for all the microwave meals he put up with, so I could spend more time writing. I am extremely grateful!

About the Author

The Holy Spirit has helped Jamie get through many *very difficult* times in her life. He has given her the desire to study the Word, share it and pray faithfully. He has opened doors for her in many amazing ways to let people know that He loves them. She stays ready and willing to do what she can, because He is worth it!

Jamie lives with her husband Lee in the home God promised her: a yellow two story, Craftsman house with teal green shutters, white picket fences and lots of flowers in Applegate, Kalamazoo, Michigan.

CPSIA information can be obtained at www.ICGtesting.com
Printed in the USA
LVOW04s0830141214

418593LV00009B/36/P